BASS
FISHING

BASS
FISHING

GALLERY BOOKS
An imprint of W.H. Smith Publishers Inc.
112 Madison Avenue
New York, New York 10016

A QUINTET BOOK
produced for
GALLERY BOOKS
An imprint of W.H. Smith Publishers Inc.
112 Madison Avenue
New York, New York 10016

ISBN 0-8317-0694-5

This book was designed and produced by
Quintet Publishing Limited
6 Blundell Street
London N7 9BH

CREATIVE DIRECTOR: Peter Bridgewater
ART DIRECTOR: Ian Hunt
DESIGNER: Sara Nunan
PROJECT EDITOR: Sally Harper
EDITOR: Elizabeth Nicholson
ILLUSTRATOR: Danny McBride

Typeset in Great Britain by
Central Southern Typesetters, Eastbourne
Manufactured in Hong Kong by Regent Publishing Services Limited
Printed in Hong Kong by Leefung-Asco Printers Limited

CONTENTS

INTRODUCTION

The surface of the water exploded upwards as the hefty golden-brown fish left its normal environment. The fish made a head-slashing attempt to dislodge this thing that it had thought was a minnow but that now had proven to be something quite different.

The yellow, black-dotted rooster-tail lure remained firmly hooked in the smallmouth's bony upper lip, as the angler met the fish's surge with an adequately taut line.

As the bass fell back into the water it bulled its way downstream toward a section of weed bed. Monofilament line was stripped off the reel as the fish increased the distance between itself and the angler. Gradually the fisherman applied the flexible tension of his rod to halt the fish's run.

Again the smallmouth cleared the surface of the water, but again the lure held in place. This time the fish returned to the water with a bit less strength left in it. The angler began to gain back the line that the fish had stolen on its previous run, and more.

The next jump into the air was less forceful. The body of the fish didn't entirely clear the surface of the water before it slid back under. More monofilament was wound about the spool of the reel, guiding the tired fish to the side of the boat.

As the three-pound (1.4kg) bass lay nearly spent next to the boat, the angler took just a moment to admire the coloring, the lines, the majesty of this creature before slipping the hook free of the fish's lip with one tug of his long-nosed pliers. Gently the angler moved the fish back and forth through the water, running the life-restoring element over the fish's gills.

Before long, the bass began to struggle to be free of the fisherman's grasp, its efforts growing stronger by the second. As the angler released it, the bass sent a splash of water into the man's face and was gone into the depths.

The angler checked that the fish was indeed gone under its own power. He wiped the water droplets from his face, made certain that line and lure were still intact, and sent a new cast to another likely smallmouth haunt.

"Inch for inch and pound for pound, the gamest fish that swims," was how James Henshall described the black bass in his monumental 1881 work *Book of the Black Bass.* This is the book to which many writers have since traced the beginnings of modern-day bass fishing. Even before the book was published, there was lively debate about the relative merits of bass over trout or northern pike or any other fish. More than a hundred years of angling history have not changed a thing. The argument still carries on in tackle shops, at sportsmen's meetings, and wherever anglers gather.

There will probably never be total agreement on which fish is the best, but the black bass is the most popular. It is readily available in one species or another in a wide variety of waters. It can be fished for in many different ways, and it is an active feeder that will give most every angler some action. For all these reasons the black bass is the most popular gamefish in America. At least half of all American anglers number the black bass as one of their prey.

The following pages were written for the 99 per cent of those bass fishermen who are of average standard. The top one per cent of our ranks (the pros, the masters) can recite everything that is in all the books ever written on the subject. Bass fishing encompasses a vast field of knowledge, which every angler adapts to his own circumstances. As a rule, he also adds to his knowledge with growing experience.

This book has been written on the basis that an understanding of the fish, its life, its habits, its motivations and its environment will lead to more fishing success, as well as to a greater appreciation of both the fish and the sport. Even in the sections that discuss the most high-tech, modern lures, you will find brief insights into the black bass. I hope the book may serve as a firm foundation for a lifetime of learning about a truly magnificent fish.

ABOVE

The beginnings of a lifetime of fishing: a farm pond, a spincasting rig, a float and a largemouth bass.

A HISTORY OF BASS FISHING

"This book owes its origin to a long-cherished desire on the part of the author, to give to the black bass its proper place among game fishes, and to create among anglers, and the public generally, an interest in a fish that has never been so fully appreciated as its merits deserve, because of the want of suitable tackle for its capture, on the one hand, and a lack of information regarding its habits and economic value on the other."

With that incredibly long sentence, James A. Henshall began his *Book of the Black Bass,* the first thorough study of a true American fish and sport. Native Americans had fished for bass since they first discovered that fish was good to eat. Nets, spears, hooks, lines and crude rods had all been developed for the purpose of catching fish. Writings by the earliest explorers of North America contain accounts of fishing for many different species, particularly bass.

In Henshall's day, articles about bass were appearing in many magazines. Henshall himself had contributed to publications such as *Forest and Stream* and the *Chicago Field*. However, his book was the first attempt to bring together all contemporary knowledge on the subject. Thus, it played a parental role for the sport that today involves millions upon millions of anglers.

Although Henshall spent a great deal of the early part of his book on the scientific aspects of the bass, it is clear from his writing that he was first and foremost a fisherman.

Soon after he completed his book, Henshall designed the forerunner of today's bait-casting rod. The eight-foot three-inch (2.5m) wooden rod, manufactured by the Orvis company, was intended primarily for fishing with live bait. Anglers of the day combined it with the recently developed Kentucky reel and it became extremely popular.

Henshall expressed his reasons for designing this rod in his book:

"In order to realize Black Bass fishing in its perfection, suitable tackle must be employed. Fishing for Brook Trout with a beanpole for a rod, and a piece of raw meat for bait, would not be considered sport in the true meaning of the term, nor should the pursuit of the Black Bass, under similar conditions, be so regarded; yet the methods of Black Bass angling heretofore described by our angling authors, and practised by most anglers, are open to the same objections ... Ten years ago, a person entering a tackle shop in a Western town, and inquiring for Bass tackle, would be presented with a rod from twelve to sixteen feet long, weighing from one to two pounds; a large brass reel, with a handle like a coffee-mill crank; a line like a chalk line and a large ungainly hook with a single bend – and all this formidable array of clumsy apparatus to do battle with such a thoroughbred and noble foe as the Black Bass!

... Those enthusiastic and observant anglers, who learned from experience that there was a want not supplied in Black Bass rods, as offered by the trade, and who possessed sufficient ingenuity, constructed their own rods and fished in their own way; and as these worthy souls were generally regarded as authority in the respective localities on the subject of Black Bass fishing, and not without reason, their particular style of rod was adopted in their particular locality as the 'perfect bass rod'."

Although greeted enthusiastically by the angling community, the Henshall Rod had a very short-lived period of popularity, because in 1885 James M. Clark unveiled his much more manageable, six-foot (1.8m) bamboo Chicago Rod. This new bait-casting rod, fitted with a Kentucky reel, gave the fisherman entirely new powers to hurl and retrieve his plugs across the water. By the dawning of the 1890s, it had become rare to see the Henshall Rod still in use.

The Chicago Rod marked the beginning of a surge in popularity for the artificial plug and a huge growth for American fishing tackle manufacturers. However, the plug can trace its ancestry back nearly a full century more, to the early 1800s. The Phantom Minnow was a metal-headed, metal-finned, silk-bodied minnow imitation, somewhat similar to many of today's stick minnows. English-made, it was available in about a dozen different lengths through the 1940s.

America waited until the 1840s to produce its own commercially manufactured bait. This first artificial lure was the Spoon lure, produced by Julio T. Buel. It consisted of a spoon blade and spinner body, to which the fisherman attached his own hooks.

The first known lure that included anything other than metal in its construction was invented by Riley Haskell and patented in 1859. In schematics, it resembled today's stick minnow, but had only one double-hook firmly attached at the rear. There is no record of the lure ever having been commercially produced.

A moonlit night, a jitterbug and some fine bass water can make for memories that will last a lifetime.

BELOW

*The end of a hard-fought
battle, as the angler nets a
farm-pond largemouth that
went for his bassbug.*

ABOVE

*A pair of fat, fall smallmouth
bass fell victim to an
imitation crayfish.*

In 1876 H.C. Brush patented and began producing Brush's Floating Spinners, which consisted of a wooden or cork float painted red and mounted in the center of a spinner blade. Although the lure was basically a spinner and not a plug, it was the first recorded, commercially produced lure to incorporate wood as a body material.

Lure innovation was somewhat stagnant for the next 15 years or so, but by the closing decade of the

1800s, carved wooden minnows (the first true plugs) were being produced by several lure manufacturers. Carved wooden frogs, crayfish and mice soon followed, as did rubber minnows.

In the early 1900s, many variations on this bait were introduced by emerging lure manufacturers. Names like Heddon, South Bend and Creek Chub were becoming well known to bass anglers across the country, all of whom were eager to try the latest miracle lures.

Of course, there were many unsuccessful ideas tried out in these early days . . . a rubber mouse covered with real mouse fur . . . the Magnifying Glass Minnow Tube (a glass tube into which the angler inserted a live minnow) . . . a lure that sent up a stream of water as it was retrieved . . . and a lure filled with "edible matter" that dissolved in the water.

However, the movement towards our modern fishing wonders was definitely under way. Even in some of the failed designs, the basic concepts behind some of today's best equipment can be found.

The sport of bass fishing has come a long way in a relatively short time. A century ago, Henshall felt the need to fight for the bass's right to be called a game fish. Today the black bass is the primary quarry of millions of American fishermen.

BASS, the Bass Anglers Sportsman Society organized in 1968, has nearly 2,300 chapters and more than 500,000 members. Smallmouth Inc., a more recent and more specialized, but swiftly growing organization that began in 1985, today has about 60 chapters and more than 10,000 members.

Bass no longer need their honor as a game fish defended.

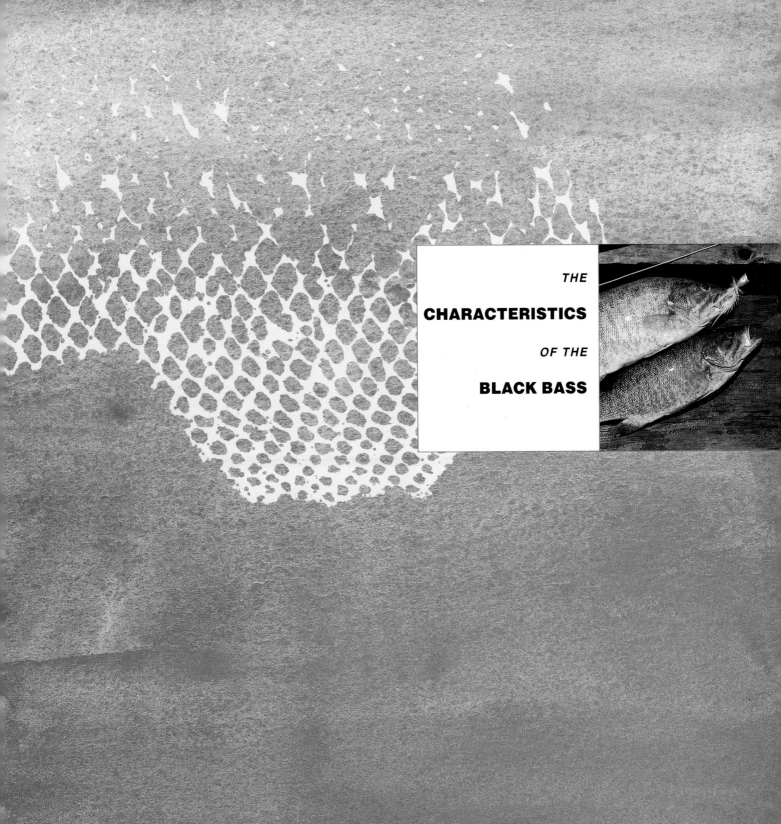

THE

CHARACTERISTICS

OF THE

BLACK BASS

IDENTIFYING FEATURES OF BASS

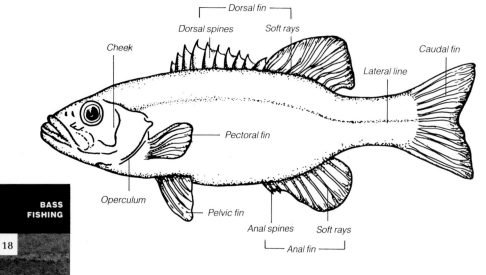

Cheek

Dorsal fin

Dorsal spines Soft rays

Caudal fin

Lateral line

Pectoral fin

Operculum

Pelvic fin

Anal spines Soft rays

Anal fin

~ Guadalupe bass (*Micropterus treculi*).

~ Redeye bass (*Micropterus coosae*).

~ Suwannee bass (*Micropterus notius*).

For many generations, popular knowledge agreed with James Henshall that there were only two species of *Micropterus,* the small-mouthed and the large-mouthed, of which the former could show some minor regional variations.

Today, researchers have revealed that there are actually six distinct species:

~ Largemouth bass (*Micropterus salmoides*), which is divided into two strains, the Florida largemouth (*Micropterus salmoides floridanus*) and the northern largemouth (*Micropterus salmoides*). The Florida subspecies grows a bit faster and larger. However, for the fisherman on the water and thus for the purposes of this book, the distinction (which requires laboratory counts of scales and vertebrae) is really of no consequence. We will refer to all largemouth bass as simply that.

~ Smallmouth bass (*Micropterus dolomieui*).

~ Spotted bass (*Micropterus punctulatus*), which is divided into two subspecies, the Alabama spotted bass (*Micropterus punctulatus henshalli*) and the Wichita spotted bass (*Micropterus punctulatus wichitae*). Again, the division has little relevance when on the water.

The final three are restricted in their range and not readily available to most anglers. The Guadalupe bass is found in rivers of south-central Texas; the redeye bass is located only in some rivers of western North and South Carolina, Georgia and Alabama; the Suwannee bass inhabits the Suwannee and a few other rivers in south-west Georgia and north-central Florida. We will offer only brief descriptions of these species in this book.

The largemouth bass is the most widespread of all the species, due mostly to the help of man, both intended and otherwise. The species today is found throughout the continental United States, southern Canada and northern Mexico. It has also been transplanted to most of the other continents across the globe, because of its ability to adapt and prosper in any bass habitat.

The smallmouth bass prospers only slightly less than the largemouth and in nearly as wide a range of habitats. Every one of the continental United States can today claim a population of smallmouth bass, but the species is still found in the greatest numbers in its original range. That area extends from the East Coast west into Texas and Minnesota, and from southern Canada south into eastern Texas through Georgia.

The spotted bass, also known as the Kentucky bass, occurs primarily within its native range from the western reaches of the Mid-Atlantic states west into Oklahoma and from Ohio, Indiana and Illinois south to near the Gulf of Mexico. Several reservoirs in California also support populations that were introduced there.

(Note: the color and pattern of most fish species varies significantly from one body of water to the next, depending upon many factors. Therefore, the following descriptions of the black bass species should be taken as a general guideline for identification.)

THE LARGEMOUTH BASS

A deep-bodied fish with a gaping mouth, the largemouth bass is mottled olive to dark green on its back with some golden flecks; silvery to greenish yellow on its sides with a dark lateral line; olive to greenish yellow on its head.

The rear of its jaw extends well beyond the rear of its eye. The pectoral fins have 14 to 15 flexible or soft rays (supporting structures in a fin); the dorsal fin has 12 to 13, with 10 spines; and the anal fin has 11, with three spines. The dorsal, caudal and anal fins are olive green. The dorsal and anal fins have no scales at their bases, but between the anal and caudal fins there are 24 to 30 rows of scales.

The lateral line extends from the opercle (gill cover) to the base of the caudal fins, covering that distance with 58 to 79 rows of scales. From seven to 10 rows of scales lie above the lateral line, while 13 to 19 lie below.

The largemouth bass is the most adaptable member of the bass family. It is found in every aquatic habitat from small streams to the largest reservoirs, and almost everything in between.

The largemouth bass has a longer lifespan in the northern part of its range, where it survives to about 16 years at its oldest. However it reaches greater size in the south. The largest largemouth on record with the National Freshwater Fishing Hall of Fame, based in Hayward, Wisconsin, remains George Perry's 22-pound, 4-ounce (10.1kg) monster. It was hauled from Montgomery Lake in Georgia on June 2, 1932.

IDENTIFYING DIFFERENT TYPES OF BASS

LARGEMOUTH BASS

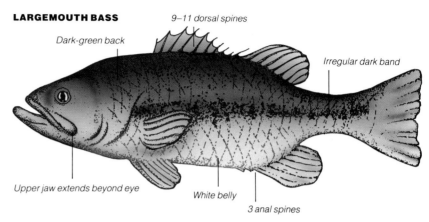

9–11 dorsal spines
Dark-green back
Irregular dark band
Upper jaw extends beyond eye
White belly
3 anal spines

SMALLMOUTH BASS

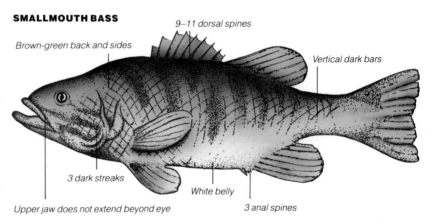

9–11 dorsal spines
Brown-green back and sides
Vertical dark bars
3 dark streaks
White belly
Upper jaw does not extend beyond eye
3 anal spines

SPOTTED BASS

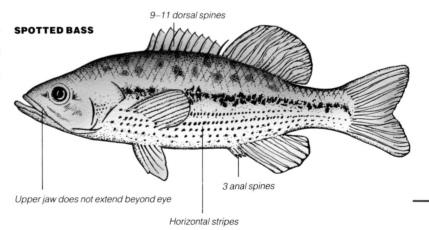

9–11 dorsal spines
Upper jaw does not extend beyond eye
3 anal spines
Horizontal stripes

THE SMALLMOUTH BASS

The smallmouth bass is visually unlike all the other black bass species in three basic ways: true to its name, the species has a smaller mouth; it also has no darker stripe along its side; and thirdly, it has more soft rays (13 to 15) in its dorsal fin.

More slender than the largemouth bass, the smallmouth is dark olive on its back with some golden flecks; brownish to greenish yellow, with darker mottling, on its sides; olive to greenish yellow on its head; and has a white underside speckled with dark brown to black.

The rear of its jaw extends no further back than the rear of its eye. The pectoral fins have 16 to 18 flexible rays; the dorsal fin has 13 to 15, with 10 spines; and the anal fin has 11, with three spines. The dorsal, caudal and anal fins are brownish, flecked with black. The dorsal and anal fins have scales at their bases, and between the anal and caudal fins there are 28 to 31 rows of scales.

The lateral line extends from the opercle to the base of the caudal fins, covering that distance with 67 to 79 rows of scales. From 10 to 14 rows of scales lie above the lateral line, while 19 to 24 lie below.

Records at the National Fresh Water Fishing Hall of Fame hold an 11-pound, 15-ounce (5.4kg) smallmouth bass as the largest member of its species that has been reported. It was taken July 9, 1955, by David Hayes on Dale Hollow Lake in Kentucky.

The smallmouth bass has fared almost as well as has its largemouth cousin. But it requires a more exacting habitat of cool streams and rivers with relatively clear water and a rocky, gravelly bottom or deep, cool lakes and reservoirs with similar conditions.

A rare subspecies of the smallmouth, the Neosho smallmouth bass (*Micropterus dolomieui velox*), occurs in the upper reaches of the river of the same name and in other feeders of the Arkansas River in Arkansas, Missouri and Oklahoma. It is thinner than other smallmouth and has a bulldog-like lower jaw that protrudes beyond its upper jaw.

THE SPOTTED BASS

The spotted bass is generally identifiable by the rows of spots below the lateral line on its side that gives it its name. It is dark olive on its back, with some golden flecks; olive to greenish yellow, with a line of irregular, darker patches that form a broken band along the lateral line on its sides; several rows of darker spots below the lateral line; olive to greenish yellow on its head.

The rear of its jaw extends no further back than the middle of its eye. The pectoral fins have 15 to 16 flexible rays; the dorsal fin has 12 to 13, with 10 spines; and the anal fin has 10, with three spines. The dorsal, caudal and anal fins are brownish olive. The dorsal and anal fins have scales at their bases,

ABOVE

The largemouth bass is both the most widespread and the largest of the black bass

≈

and between the anal and caudal fins there are 22 to 28 rows of scales.

The lateral line extends from the opercle to the base of the caudal fins, covering that distance with 59 to 74 rows of scales. From eight to 10 rows of scales lie above the lateral line, while 15 to 20 lie below.

The spotted bass is much more restricted to streams, rivers and man-made habitats than are the smallmouth and largemouth species. It has never prospered in natural lakes. The spotted bass prefers rocky, deeper areas with more current than the water favored by the largemouth, and it likes warmer, slower areas than does the smallmouth.

The largest spotted bass recorded by the National Fresh Water Fishing Hall of Fame is the 8-pound, 15-ounce (4kg) specimen caught on March 18, 1978, by Philip Terry Jr on Lewis Smith Lake in Alabama.

THE GUADALUPE BASS

The Guadalupe bass has irregular, vertical patches of olive, mottled across a field of lighter green on its sides, which fades into an off-white color on its underside.

The rear of its jaw extends no further back than the middle of its eye. The pectoral fins have 13 to 16 flexible rays; the dorsal fin has 19 to 21, with 10 spines; and the anal fin has 12, with three spines. The dorsal, caudal and anal fins are brownish olive. The dorsal and anal fins have scales at their bases, and between the anal and caudal fins there are 20 to 25 rows of scales.

The lateral line extends from the opercle to the base of the caudal fins, covering that distance with 63 to 68 rows of scales. From eight to nine rows of scales lie above the lateral line, while 15 to 17 lie below.

THE REDEYE BASS

The redeye bass looks a great deal like the smallmouth, however it can be clearly distinguished by its deep red eyes and fins.

The rear of its jaw extends no further back than the middle of its eye. The dorsal and anal fins of the redeye bass have scales at their bases, and between the anal and caudal fins there are varying rows of scales.

The lateral line extends from the opercle to the base of the caudal fin, covering that distance with 67 to 72 rows of scales. From nine to 10 rows of scales lie above the lateral line, while 15 to 27 lie below.

There are two races of redeye bass: the shoal or Apalachicola, and the Alabama.

The largest redeye bass recorded at the National Fresh Water Fishing Hall of Fame weighed 8-pound, 3-ounces (3.7kg). It was taken on October 23, 1977, on the Flint River in Georgia by David Hubbard.

THE SUWANNEE BASS

Suwannee bass were first discovered in the early 1940s in Florida's Ichtucknee Springs. They have since been found in several other Florida waters, including the Suwannee River.

The species looks much like the redeye and spotted bass, except for a noticeable blue tint throughout its underside. It is a relatively small species, with most individuals growing to less than a foot (0.3m) in length and less than a pound (0.5kg) in weight. However, the National Fresh Water Fishing Hall of Fame shows a 3-pound, 9-ounce (1.6kg) Suwannee bass as the largest on record. Laverne Norton landed the fish on October 6, 1984, on the Ochlockonee River in Georgia.

SPAWNING

All the black bass share many common spawning and nesting characteristics.

Bass spawn in the spring, when water temperatures begin to move up past 60 degrees Fahrenheit (14°C). The spring spawning urge in a bass is set off by both water temperature and photoperiod, but water temperature is a more easily measured gauge.

Photoperiod is the proportion of the day during which the bass is exposed to sunlight. As the daylight hours grow longer through the spring and early summer, so does the photoperiod. This process affects the temperature of different bodies of water in different ways. Small, shallow ponds, for example,

will heat up much earlier in the year than large, deep reservoirs.

As a result, pond and small-stream bass will usually begin the spawn much earlier than their large-water counterparts. They will also conclude their spawning activity earlier. In the northernmost part of the bass's range the spawn may last for only a month, while it may extend for almost six months in the Deep South.

The male is the first to move into the spawning grounds, making the relocation well before the water temperature has reached the spawning levels. He begins work on the nest site, a task in which the female will join him later.

The fish build their spawning nests in anything from half a foot (15cm) to 25 feet (7.5m) of water. However, where habitat is suitable, most of the nests will be found in water that is less than six feet (1.8m) deep.

Bass generally use structures like stumps and larger rocks as protection for the nest. Largemouth bass have shown a preference for a sandy bottom

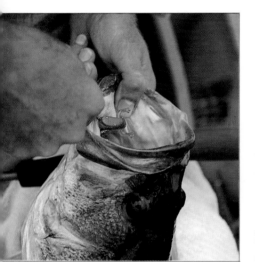

for their nests, while smallmouth bass tend toward more gravelly bottoms, and spotted bass will usually build closer to weedy cover than the other two species.

The nest is a shallow, circular depression scooped out of the substrate. Its size can range from less than a foot (0.3m) to more than four feet (1.2m) in diameter.

Although many bass nests are often found in the same sheltered area on a body of water, none will generally be closer than six feet (1.8m) away from its neighbor. This "social" distance apparently allows enough space for the bass to avoid constant squabbles among themselves, which would waste vital energy that they need to fend off the truly destructive intruders.

When the water temperature rises to within the spawning range, the female lays her eggs over the nest, with the male spreading his fertile milt over them. This is a glue-like substance which adheres the eggs to the substrate of the nest as they sink to the bottom.

From 2,000 to 7,000 eggs per pound (0.5kg) of body weight are laid by the average female bass. However, she lays only a few hundred of them at any one time, and her total clutch may be divided over several nests, through spawnings with several different males. In addition, eggs from several females can often be found in a single nest, all resulting from spawning with the male that guards that particular depression.

The female bass will stay close to the nest for a couple of days after laying her eggs. But the male will stay on until the eggs hatch, guarding them from the predators that lurk nearby. These predators include turtles, salamanders, frogs, crayfish, panfish and some species of minnows. The male bass also maintains a fanning action over the nest with his tail to prevent a build-up of oxygen-choking silt.

If something happens to remove the male from this sentry duty, the nest and its contents will be lost. Catching the male during this protective period is quite easy to do, as the fish fights off and physically removes anything that nears the nest. Not to return him immediately to the water would amount to nothing less than destroying the nest itself.

If all goes well, the eggs hatch in two to 10 days. Higher temperatures speed up the process, while lower temperatures slow it down. The young fry begin to feed on microscopic creatures in the water almost as soon as they leave the eggs. The male stands guard over his brood for several more days, until they begin to disperse on their own.

At that point the male begins gradually to lose his protective instincts and to return to his former predatory ways. The last few stragglers may become his first meal since he began his vigil over the nest.

During their first few years the bass tend to live as school fish. They do not necessarily travel with all of their own siblings, but do generally stay in schools of fish of about the same size. As their growth continues they become loners, seeking out a spot where they may well spend much of their lives, unless driven off by a larger fish. Spawning and drastic environmental changes are the only factors that will carry them away from this spot for long.

THE SENSES

Black bass make wider use of all of their senses than do many other fish species. Their combination of sharp vision, acute smell, discerning taste and enhanced hearing is what has made them the superior predator they are. It has also made them into excellent gamefish.

Which sense is most important in locating prey, and is thus of utmost importance to the angler, is debatable. An understanding of them all is crucial to angling success.

Bass, like nearly all fish, are near-sighted. In water, where visibility is usually limited to relatively close distances, this is not a handicap.

On the other hand, with their eyes located on the sides of their heads, bass have a much greater field of vision than we humans. Each of the bass's eyes can see nearly 180 degrees (a half-circle) on its side of the body. This range is somewhat tilted towards the front of the fish, leaving a blind spot to the immediate rear and creating an overlap in front of the fish.

This optical arrangement gives the bass its greatest depth perception in the overlapping zone in front, but its clearest vision is at a right angle to the eye. Thus a prey or lure passing beside the fish will quickly attract its attention, and the fish is able to determine the distance of a prey that it is striking to the front.

Bass definitely see in color, although their water-filtered perception of color is different from our air-filtered sight. First, we must understand that all colors are actually reflections of various wavelengths of light. Every surface absorbs certain wavelengths and reflects others. These wavelengths vary across a spectrum from blue (shortest wavelengths) through green, yellow and orange to red (longest wavelengths).

Water complicates this process by filtering out certain wavelengths at specific depths. The longest wavelengths are absorbed fastest, so the reds are eliminated from the spectrum very near the surface, even in the clearest of water. The shortest wavelengths (the blues) travel the deepest into the water. Obviously this filtering process has a great impact on the colors of our lures at different depths. How-

ever bass preferences are still being widely studied and debated.

Given the murky conditions of even the clearest underwater environment, movement may well be more important than color in attracting the bass's attention. The predatory, opportunistic nature of the bass leads the fish to examine almost any movement within its field of vision for fear of missing an easy meal.

The bass's eye is designed also to adjust gradually to changes in light intensity. In place of the iris, found in humans, the bass's eye has receptor cells of two types (cones for bright light and rods for lower levels of light) which it can move toward and away from the surface of the eye.

The process takes much longer than the almost instantaneous adjustment of the human iris, and the bass goes through two daily periods of adjustment, at dawn and dusk.

Hearing is much more complex in bass than it is in humans. Not only does the fish have ears on the sides of its head that are sensitive to high-frequency, long-range sounds, but it also sports what is known as the lateral line along the sides of its body. This organ, which is made up of a series of canals and pods of tiny hairs, is particularly sensitive to the low-frequency sounds of movement in the water close by. The lateral line can give the bass enough information about an object moving within a few feet of it to enable it to strike that object without ever seeing it.

The ears and lateral line between them provide the bass with an exceptional range of "hearing". In addition, sound in the water travels five to six times faster than it does in the air, and carries over greater distances.

The sense of smell in a bass, as in most fish, operates when water moves through its nostrils and across internal olfactory organs. The more water that moves across them, the better the fish's sense of smell.

Bass smell a wide range of odors in the water, but smell is probably of most use to them as a long-range sensor of prey. For exact locating, hearing and sight take over.

Taste comes into play after the bass has located and attacked its prey. The fish has taste buds on its tongue and palate, as we do, but it also has them on its lips and nose. Consequently, the bass can begin to taste an object without ever taking it into its mouth. That might offer some food for thought for the angler.

BELOW

The black bass has an incredible collection of survival instincts and senses, an understanding of which will boost your fishing success.

TACKLE *AND*
TECHNIQUE

RIGS

One of the most endearing qualities about the average black bass (not necessarily the mega-lunker) is the fish's enthusiasm for just about any lure or bait offered on nearly any freshwater rig. Bait-casting, spin-fishing, fly-fishing, ice-fishing tip-up, cane pole and hand-line have all taken bass. They all continue to take bass.

Of this myriad of rigs, bait-casting, spin-fishing and fly-fishing are the clear majority favorites.

For many years, bait-casting was closely akin to the work of the Devil. It seemed to be the norm to find your line transformed into a fierce, backlashing bird's nest. Precious fishing time was then spent in untangling the mess, very often with the help of a knife blade. This always seemed to coincide with the times when the bass went into a feeding frenzy.

The backlashes occurred because of an inherent problem in the design of the reel, which holds its spool of line at right angles to the rod. This required

the angler to apply thumb pressure on the spool at the instant the lure hit the water, to prevent extra line from zipping off the reel. A second's delay would produce the most mind-boggling tangles.

Manufacturers were perhaps slow to respond to the problem, but they have now done so. Today's bait-casting rig is a smooth-actioned, space-age mechanism, complete with at least one anti-backlash device.

That is not to say that bait-casting has become the easiest of fishing methods. It still falls somewhere between the much easier spin-fishing and the more difficult fly-fishing. However, for accuracy in casting, no other method can match the bait-casting rig in the hands of a master.

Spin-fishing (a post-World War II invention) is easier for the beginner and casual angler to master, with its forward-facing spool of line and nearly automatic, line-controlling metal bail. Although the spin-fishing reel will throw up a backlash or two now and again, its open-face design generally makes it much easier and faster to right the situation.

To cast with spin-fishing gear, the angler simply hooks the line immediately off the reel spool with his index finger, flips the bail to its open position, hauls back and lets fly on the cast. As the lure hits the water, a simple half-turn or less on the reel handle will spring the bail into the closed position, preventing additional line from streaming off the spool. Even when the angler misses his cue, and allows more line to strip out after the lure has hit the water, the line generally passes through the eyelets of the rod without backlashing at all.

Spin-fishing reels, however, are prone occasionally to wrap the line about their inner workings. This means removing the spool and unwinding the line that has fouled, which is a simple procedure.

A variation of the spin-fishing reel that is even easier to use is the spin-cast reel. This is widely thought of as a rod for children to use when they are beginning. The open-face/bail arrangement of the spin-fishing reel is replaced by a closed-face mechanism controlled by a large thumb-button at the rear of the reel. The spin-cast has the advantage of being easy to use, but it does not have the accuracy of the bait-casting rig or the distance of spin-fishing gear.

Both today's bait-casting and spin-fishing reels are equipped with drag-setting controls. Drag is the tension that the closed bail applies to the line. Light drag translates into less tension; tighter drag offers more resistance to the fish at the other end of the line.

RODS

Bait-casting and spin-fishing rods come in an assortment of weights which indicate the stiffness and strength of the rods. The primary weights are ultralight, light, medium and heavy. With each passing year, manufacturers are offering more intermediate weights, such as light-medium.

Ultralights are small, feather-light, highly flexible rods. They are intended to give the feel of lunker-battling to any fish that is hooked. Their tiny reels are equipped with the lightest of monofilament line, usually two- or four-pound-test. Some manufacturers have moved beyond the ultralight into the super-ultralight to satisfy the growing demand for this exciting type of fishing that is winning more advocates each year.

Light rods are slightly less flexible, a bit heavier to hold and longer than the ultralights. They allow for exciting handling of the fish, on heavier line in the four- to ten-pound-test range on their larger reels.

Medium action rods are less flexible and light in

ABOVE

Baitcasting gear is the top choice among many professional bass fishermen, but for the beginner it can be tough to master.

LEFT

The three most popular methods of bass fishing are baitcasting (left), spinfishing (right) and fly fishing (top).

the hand, but offer more control over the fish. They use heavier lines (up to about 20-pound-test) on their larger reels. They are intended for larger fish. When the bass pro on television "horses" a lunker over the side of the boat and the rod hardly bends, you know he is using at least a medium action rod.

Heavy-action rods are designed for battling the largest fish on the heaviest line (more than 20-pound-test). They are stiff, heavy-handed affairs that, for most bass fishing, would hardly flinch at the fish's tug.

As you may have already guessed, my own preferences are the ultralight and light gear. The ultralight is superior for small-stream fishing, where the chances of a truly giant bass are minimal, but where many average fish can provide superb fights on this rig.

The light gear is my choice for river, lake and reservoir fishing, although this choice carries with it some inherent problems in heavy weedbeds and tight structure.

LINE

The most important aspect of any rig is the proper matching of rod, reel, line and lure. Most reels today come with an indication as to which action rod they most closely match, but the choice of line remains wide open.

Manufacturers have made great strides in recent years in improving monofilament fishing line. They have increased the strength while decreasing the diameter, and have developed an incredible array of lines that are "invisible" in certain underwater conditions. They have even rid us of the accursed memory problem, whereby the line continues to coil even when off the spool.

For the average fisherman, differences in monofilament come down to a few basic points:

~ Strength. The pound-test measure provided on the package is a reliable indicator of the strength of line. Often it will be stronger than indicated, but it would be very rare for it to be less than the quoted strength. Twenty-pound-test is stronger than ten-pound-test, which is stronger than six-pound-test, and so on.

~ Visibility. This issue has become more complicated with the introduction of lines of almost every color. Some are easier for the angler to see, while others purport to be less visible to the fish.

~ Resistance to abrasion. As you fish with the line, some of its strength will be lost through abrasion with obstructions. Some lines are more resistant to this than others.

~ Limpness. How easily does the line bend and crimp? Too much limpness makes for a poor-casting line, while too little means that excess line will flee the reel with each cast, and you will have tangles.

The following are examples of matched rods, reels, lines, and lures:

~ An ultralight reel on an ultralight rod with two- to four-pound-test line and ⅟32 to ½-ounce (1–14g) lures.

~ A light reel on a light rod with four- to eight-pound-test line and ⅛ to ⅝-ounce (3.5–17.5g) lures.

~ A medium reel on a medium rod with eight- to ten-pound-test line with ¼ to ¾-ounce (7–21g) lures.

~ A heavy reel on a heavy rod with 12- to 20-pound-test line and ½ to one-ounce (14–28g) lures.

ABOVE
Spinfishing is often a good choice for the casual angler or the fisherman who spends most of his time on smaller, shallower waters.

FLY-FISHING

Fly-fishing, long the bastion of elitist trout anglers, is gaining popularity in the bass-angling ranks today. You won't find the tournament pros bouncing delicate hairbugs across the lily pads, but you will see more and more fishermen taking bass in epic fly-fishing battles.

For generations, fly-fishing has been bathed in undeserved myth and mystique. Although it is an extremely exciting and intimate way to catch a fish, fly-fishing still amounts to a rod, reel, line and lure. With practice anyone can master the techniques.

LEFT
Ultralight gear will make every bass feel like a lunker.

Fly rods for bass need to be rather stiffer than those used for trout. The lures are larger and the fish's mouth is harder, necessitating the extra hook-setting power.

Fly rods are generally longer and more flexible than either bait-casting or spin-fishing rods. The level-wind spool type of fly reel is a relatively simple device, although automatic reels are much more complicated.

The real differences in fly-fishing are that you rely on the weight of the line rather than the weight of the lure to carry the cast, and that the tension to fight the fish is created in the angler's hands rather than by the reel's drag.

Fly-fishing outfits, like the others, are rated in weights, though on a different system. One- and two-weights are ultralight; five- and six-weights are light; eight-weight is heavier (the preferred weight for bass); and nine- and ten-weights are the heavy-duty rigs for fish such as salmon and northern pike.

Lines for fly-fishing are available as floating (for dry flies and surface bass bugs), and sinking or sinking-tip (for wet flies and streamers). The lines may be either level (the same diameter along the entire length) or tapered. The latter are designed to propel as much energy as possible through the cast.

The leader, a section of monofilament line from six to nine feet (two to three metres) in length, is tied to the end of the fly line and then to the fly. The leader is tapered to its thinnest diameter (the tippet) at the fly-end. The test of this tippet must be matched to the fly that is being fished and the fish to which it is being cast. A one-pound tippet will give the smallest dry fly a delicate landing on the water's surface, but will rip under the weight of a large bassbug, not to mention a bass. A six-pound tippet would drag that same dry fly ineffectively under the surface of the water, but would handle the bassbug perfectly.

RIGHT
Fly fishing has gained acceptance as a means of catching bass and is growing in popularity.

ABOVE
The weight of the line, rather than the weight of the lure, carries the fly fisherman's cast.

A six-pound tippet is probably the minimum for bass fishing. For fishing in heavy structure, eight- to 12-pound may be the proper choice. And, for lunkers, 20-pound is not outrageous.

TROLLING

Trolling is not a major aspect of bass fishing, but it can sometimes add a few fish to the day's catch.

In late summer and early fall, for example, when the fish are seeking the cooler, more oxygenated waters of the depths, they can be found further from cover than normal. Likewise, in spring, when they move up onto the shallows for spawning, they may be more exposed than at other times.

When trolling, the angler must match his lure choice to the specific conditions he finds. Deep divers will be needed in the first situation, while floating-diving lures will meet the second challenge. On larger bodies of water, downriggers may be necessary to get the lure down to the fish. Some enthusiasts do not consider this true bass fishing.

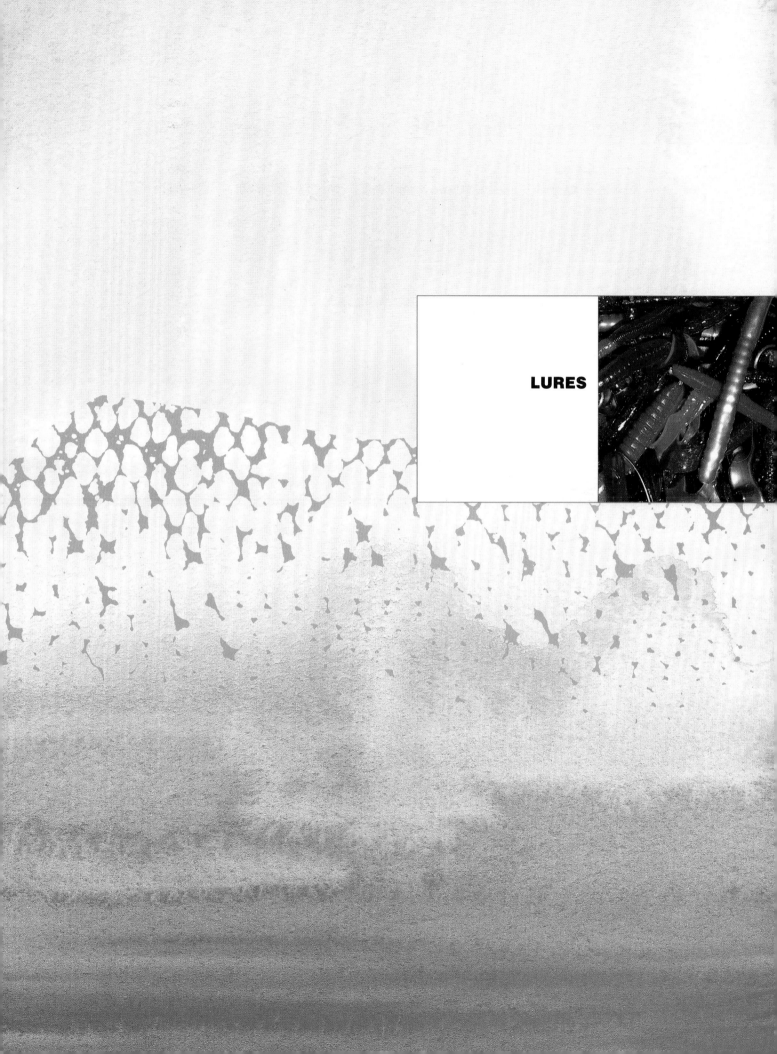

LURES

Despite the multi-million-dollar sales of lures each year, the old standby, and often the first choice, remains live bait. This includes crayfish, minnows, worms, frogs, salamanders, hellgramites and large grasshoppers. That list by no means covers all the natural items that the bass consumes, but I don't know of many anglers who would want to carry a snake, baby duckling or other such fare in their bait bucket.

Whenever you collect your own live bait, be certain that you are obeying applicable laws. Many states regulate the numbers of minnows and frogs that any one angler can have in his possession. Salamanders, which have been heavily affected by acid rain, are coming under protection as a threatened or endangered species.

MINNOWS

Artificials have been patterned after minnows more often than after any of the others on our list, and for good reason. The number one prey of the largemouth bass is the minnow.

The word "minnow" is a generic term that can apply to nearly any small fish. "Baitfish" is another common term for these small fish. Those families of minnow most often used in bass fishing include shiners, chub, stone cats and dace. They can be purchased in almost any tackle shop or bait store, but are also easy to gather in a seine net or minnow trap. Three to five inches (7.5 to 12.5cm) is the optimum length for most bass fishing, although your imagination is the limit if you are going after lunkers.

To be fished live, the minnow should be hooked through both lips, from bottom to top, with the hook protruding through the top. This will help to keep the bait lively through several casts. Other means of

hooking often cause injury to the minnow and shorten its life on the hook.

Left to its own devices, a minnow will immediately head for the nearest cover. This might be a weedbed or a large overhanging rock. The result for the angler is a snag and possibly a ripped line.

A small float will maintain some control over the minnow, while still allowing it to swim about in a natural-looking manner. If it insists on skimming the surface, a small split-shot will take it down to where bass expect to see and attack it.

The minnow can also be "threaded" onto the hook, with a large needle sold for this purpose. With the line attached, the needle is passed through the minnow, moving from mouth to anus. The end of the line is then detached from the needle and tied to the hook, which is then tugged into the anus of the minnow.

This method kills the minnow, but that is acceptable, since a minnow rigged in this manner is intended for use as a moving lure. The angler supplies the bait's motion, as he would with an artificial stick minnow (see page 41).

ABOVE
Gathering the live bait can be nearly as much fun as fishing with it. Here, Pennsylvania outdoor author Scott Weidensaul uses a seine net to catch crayfish, minnows and hellgrammites for a bass fishing trip.

RIGHT
A live shiner proved to be the right bait for this largemouth bass. Minnows are the species' favorite diet items.

CRAYFISH

As minnow is to largemouth, so crayfish is to small-mouth. Nothing catches the bronzeback like crayfish, crawfish, crawdad, or whatever you want to call them. The crustacean is also popular with the largemouth.

Live crayfish have never left me with a completely fishless day. The plastic and rubber imitations, which seem to appear in more versions every year, have proven nearly as reliable. However, success with this bait requires some understanding of the crayfish's life and habits.

Crayfish have a definite preference for the rockiest areas of any body of water. Although a few may be found under smaller rocks in gravel, larger rocks and boulders generally hold more crayfish. This is the key to finding and capturing your bait (which is best done with two anglers and a seine net) and is also a guide to where to use it.

The small crustaceans do not swim. They spend most of their time walking slowly along the bottom. When threatened, they propel themselves backwards for a short distance with a flip of the tail, but even then they remain very close to the bottom. You must fish your bait or imitation in this same way. Unless it is bouncing the bottom, rather than slicing through the water, a crayfish is not going to look natural to the bass. This applies equally to the plastic or rubber version.

Crayfish cannot grow without molting. At these times, they shed their hard armor-like shell and enter a softshell stage. The bass are aware of this relatively unprotected situation and are quick to grab any crayfish with the look of a softshell.

A live crayfish with the hardest of shells can be transformed into an appetizing softshelled beauty simply by peeling the large shell across its back. Starting from the point where the larger shell contacts the first segment of the tail, lift the shell away from the body slowly and toward the front of the crayfish. Take care not to pull too far and rip the shell, with the animal's head, from the body. With

ABOVE

Manufacturers have responded to the popularity of the crayfish as a bass bait, with a wide assortment of hard and soft plastic imitations. The most important aspect of any crayfish lure is that it mimics a live crayfish as closely as possible.

≈

FISHING WITH CRAYFISH BAIT

Crayfish do well when fished in these spots; **1.** *rows of stumps;* **2.** *fallen trees on a point;* **3.** *flooded bushes near a point;* **4.** *logs on a flat;* **5.** *isolated weed patches;* **6.** *weed pockets;* **7.** *inside weed bends;* **8.** *weed lines near the bank;* **9.** *pockets in weeds;* **10.** *wood objects caught in weeds.*

the shell sufficiently lifted from the body, break it off at the point where it contacts the crayfish's neck.

A crayfish should be hooked through a few, forward segments of its tail, with the hook protruding upwards. This will give the bait a natural appearance as it is slowly retrieved.

WORMS
≈

Worms (primarily of the nightcrawler size, in the case of bass fishing) are probably the best-known fishing bait. They are the easiest bait to obtain, coming to the surface on any rainy spring or summer night. They are available at nearly every bait or tackle shop, or even from many minute-markets. They can also be real fish-producers.

The key is to allow the worm to work in something resembling its natural movements. If it is clumped about the hook in a ball, the worm will look completely unnatural to a bass.

To find out what a worm normally looks like, drop one into some clear, shallow water. You won't see much "balling up". Instead, the worm will generally curve and elongate its body as it moves about. This is the look you want on your hook.

Insert the hook's point just in front of the thick band that might be viewed as a neck collar. Thread the worm onto the hook until there is one bend in its body along the curve of the hook. Allow the point to remain inside the worm. No more hookings should be done. The majority of the worm should be allowed to trail free to provide bass-enticing motion.

When the fish takes the bait, it may well have grabbed the non-hook end. Trying to set the hook at this point would probably result in a torn worm for you and a free lunch for the fish. Give the bass free line to run with the worm for a bit. When it stops to swallow its meal, wait a second or two and then set the hook.

Worms can be fished effectively in any live-bait rigs: free-floating/sinking, with float, with weight, with float and weight.

Not too many years ago the first plastic/rubber worms began to appear in tackle shops. They looked much like real ones and offered a few color choices. Blue was one of my favorites at the beginning of the plastic worm era. Today there are innumerable variations in color, length, shape and texture. Recent years have also seen the introduction of the scent factor, which can make a package of plastic worms smell like a candy or perfume shop.

Variety is the key. Cover the range of the rainbow, from the extremes of black to white, and throw in whatever catches your fancy, but don't worry about having every shade of every color on hand. Much has been written about the proper colors and shades to use, and most of the advice is contradictory.

GUIDE TO LIVE BAIT AND ARTIFICIALS

LIVE	ARTIFICIAL	
MINNOWS (including chubs, shiners and other small fish). Hook through back, tail or lips.	Streamers; jigs; spinnerbaits; spoons; spinners; crankbaits (floater/divers, sinker/divers, stickbaits, surface disturbers).	
WORMS (including night crawlers). Use for trout, bass and panfish. Hook through head.	Plastic worms.	
CRAYFISH Use either entire crayfish or tail only; hook through tail.	Pork rind frog on skirted jig; slow-rising and sinking/diving crankbaits; soft plastic crayfish on slider hooks or jigs.	
FROGS AND SALAMANDERS For salamander, hook through tail, front leg or lips; through thigh or lips for frog.	Soft plastic salamanders on worm hooks or jigs; weedless rubber frogs with hanging legs; pork rind frogs as trailers on weedless spoons.	
INSECTS (including grubs, caterpillars, hellgrammites, crickets and grasshoppers). Thread grubs and small caterpillars on hook; hook through collar for crickets, grasshoppers and hellgrammites.	Bass bugs; dry flies; wet flies; nymphs; terrestrials (eg ants, beetles, grasshoppers, crickets).	

Experimentation is the best method of revealing the desires of the fish in your area. Run through the spectrum, a few casts for each color, at a known bass spot, and the fish may soon guide you on what color to use that day.

The choice of length and shape will also vary with the situation. These determine the action of the plastic worm in the water. The flattened, hooked tails usually produce movements that resemble injured minnows. The long, thick tails curve their way through the water, resembling snakes or leeches. The oversized and multi-faceted tails will go through a theatrical range of motions, not related to anything in the bass's natural habitat. Nonetheless, they can be effective when the bass are in a mood to attack whatever they see, for instance in the immediate pre-spawn period.

Texture refers primarily to the softness or firmness of the plastic worms. You want a worm that will last for many casts, offering the bass a nice soft meal and allowing easy setting of the hook. But you don't want something that will look like the product of a paper shredder after only a few casts. The ideal texture strikes a balance between the two extremes.

Scented worms are aimed in fact at the bass's tasting ability. They may be an improvement on the normal-smelling worms, but I have yet to see any scientific evidence that bass prefer them.

The most important phase when fishing plastic worms is the waiting game after the bass takes the lure. Set the hook too soon and you will rip the worm harmlessly out of the fish's mouth; too late, and the bass will already have expelled the artificial.

Strikes range from very light tap-taps to fast and furious runs immediately the worm hits the water. The proven method for detecting strikes is to keep the slack out of your line as much as possible.

The most popular method of fishing plastic worms is the Texas rig. A bullet-shaped slip sinker is slipped onto the line ahead of the hook. Use a 1/0 for a 4-inch (10cm) worm, 3/0 for a 6-inch (15cm) worm and 4/0 and 7-inch (17.5cm) and longer worms. This is then tied onto the line. The point of the head is inserted into the center of the head of the worm, pushed down through the worm and brought out the side about ¼ inch (6mm) from the initial insertion point. The hook is then pulled down through the worm's head until the eye is inside the worm. Finally the hook is rotated 180 degrees, until the

point is directed back toward the worm, and inserted back into the plastic so that the barb of the hook is fully embedded.

A variation on the Texas rig is the Carolina rig, intended for waters with particularly weedy bottoms. A small split shot is added between the hook and the slip sinker, an inch to a few inches (several centimetres) ahead of the hook. This allows the slip sinker to pull along the bottom, with the worm slightly above the weeds, where the bass can see it.

A further variation on either the Texas or Carolina rigs is to add a tandem hook further back in the worm body. The eye of the second hook is looped over the first hook. The points of both hooks are then inserted into the worm body and the rig is ready to go.

A variation on the plastic worm is the plastic grub, which is a shorter, squatter version of the worm, generally with some sort of flip-tail. Hooked onto a quarter-ounce or lighter jig head, the grub can be bumped slowly along the bottom to imitate a crayfish, or retrieved like a crankbait to imitate a swimming minnow.

An array of colors, sizes, shapes and textures of grub now exists, similar to that available for plastic worms. Experimentation will again reveal the right ones for you to carry.

Plastic worms and grubs can be effective at any time of the year, but they are a critical part of the arsenal in the late fall. As the water cools, the cold-blooded bass becomes much less active and more opportunistic in its feeding habits. The slow-moving meals take on increasing appeal.

SNAKE-BAITS

A recent alternative among the plastic worm-type lures is the snake design. Rather than being a gim-

FROGS AND SALAMANDERS

Another new version of the plastic worm and pork rind baits is the salamander. These "lizards" can be fished behind a weight or floated. Both methods are generally productive in and near weedbeds. The angler will generally have to gather his own frogs and salamanders, which is quite easily done along the water's edge and in damp, marshy areas. A small-veined net will be helpful in snatching frogs, while salamanders will be found under rotting logs.

A maximum length of two to three inches (5 to 7.5cm) is optimum for frogs, while salamanders might be a bit longer. Both frogs and salamanders may be hooked through the lips. Frogs can also be hooked through a thigh, while the alternative rig for salamanders is a leg or tail.

Cast the frog or salamander to the edge of a weedbed or other cover and allow it to swim naturally. A float is often needed to keep the bait from burying itself on the bottom.

HELLGRAMMITES AND GRASSHOPPERS

Hellgrammites are the fearsome-looking aquatic larvae of dobsonflies found under rocks in many streams and rivers across the continent. Those large choppers can deliver a painful bite. I have seen them sold in the occasional bait shop, but more often have had to gather my own with a seine net.

The hellgrammite should be hooked through the collar and fished with a float. It must be kept slightly off the bottom, otherwise it will crawl under a rock and snag the line. If it tends to float too near the surface, a split-shot may be necessary to get it down where the bass expect to find it.

TOP

Try to find a color that is not represented in this collection of plastic worms, which is only a small selection of the variety available today.

ABOVE

Live crayfish are hooked through the first several sections of their tail. They are the top food choice of the smallmouth bass.

mick to attract fishermen, if not fish, the snake-bait is an imitation of a natural part of the bass diet: the water snake.

With a large, floating head and rubbery, flip-tail body, the snake-bait moves at the surface of the water and across the tops of weedbeds. The head remains out of the water, just like that of the real water snake.

Snake-baits are available in a choice of sizes, ranging up to about 12 inches (30cm). The life cycle of the snake is the best clue to the appropriate size. Most water snakes give birth to their young from August through October. The smaller, baby snake imitations will therefore be more effective during this period.

Bear in mind the natural habitat of the snake when fishing snake-baits. Weedbeds and stick-ups in areas of slower moving water are likely places to find water snakes.

As with everything else that a bass will eat, frogs, salamanders, hellgrammites and grasshoppers are all now available in effective imitations. The angler can take his pick among soft plastics, hard plastics, pork rind and bassbug mimics.

CRANKBAITS

Crank them in and their oversized lip makes them dive. Stop cranking them and they float. They, of course, are the crankbaits that first emerged in the 1930s, exploded in popularity in the 1940s, and have continued to catch bass ever since.

These bulging plastics are now available in an incredible array of colors and patterns, imitating minnows, crayfish, frogs and more. There are designs that can make these lures do just about everything but sit up and beg.

Their diving abilities lie largely in their huge lips. The larger the lip, the deeper the lure will dive. Small diameter monofilament, moderate rather than fast retrieve, and a rod tip held low during the retrieve will also send the crankbait further into the depths. The diving depth provided by the manufacturer is only a starting-point.

A mistake that many anglers make when using crankbaits (and many other lures) is to use them straight from the packaging without testing to see if they need to be tuned. Today's crankbaits are precision-made and most will function properly. However pre-fishing testing is still mandatory and tuning might be necessary.

Tuning involves adjusting the point of line connection to correct the dive of the lure, or to make it swim correctly, at the required depth. It should not roll or spin, and the line should not twist. You should be able to troll several lures without them becoming entangled.

Grasshoppers are easily collected in weedy areas, early on dew-soaked mornings following cool nights. The cold-blooded creatures are slow to escape under these conditions, until they have had a jump-start from the heat of the sunlight. They can also be gathered by stretching a nylon stocking or two for a few hours in an area that they frequent. Their spurred legs snag in the fine webbing.

Only those grasshoppers longer than two to two-and-a-half inches (5 to 6cm) should be considered for bass fishing. Hooked on a light hook, through the collar, the grasshopper should be fished on the surface, near weedbed and other bass cover. A fly rod can make the use of grasshopper both easier and more exciting.

It is important that you do not shave the side of the plastic-lipped lure. Also, avoid bending the metal lip as this can cause water to get inside the body of the lure and ruin it.

Do not bend the front eyelet any more than necessary because if it becomes loose the lure will cease to be tunable, and could start to leak. Pulling the line-tie eyelet from the front and twisting it is another way to ruin the lure, or put it out of tune.

You should carry out the test in calm water. The tuning procedure is a matter of bending the line-tie eyelet in the direction opposite to the lure's line of travel. If the lure runs to your right as you reel it in, you must bend the eyelet slightly to the left, and vice versa. As mentioned above, moving the eyelet too much may ruin the lure, so make minimal adjustments each time until you have the effect you want.

If the lure has an eyelet embedded in lip, you should adjust it using needle-nose pliers to bend the eyelet very slightly toward the side of the lip. If the lure runs to the right coming toward you, one prong of the pliers should be on the left of the lip and the other prong on the right of the line-tie eyelet. If it runs to the left, they should be the other

way round. Test the action and tune again until lure runs true.

In the case of lures with a metal lip and connecting link, tuning is done by bending the connecting link at the position of the clasp, at the mid-joint. This can usually be done by hand. If the lure is running to the right, put your thumb on the clasp, and bend the top of the connecting link slightly to the left with your index finger. Check the action of the lure and retune if necessary. If the lure is running to the left, bend the top of the link the other way.

Tuning a lure with an eyelet on the nose again requires needle-nose pliers. With the pliers pointing upwards, pincer the line-tie eyelet from either side. If the lure is swimming to the left when coming towards you, bend the eyelet slightly and very gently to the right. If the lure is swimming to the right, do the reverse. Test the lure and adjust as necessary until it runs true.

STICK MINNOWS

These floating-diving minnows (also known by other names such as slim minnows) can be wonderfully effective in shallow water. Their story began for bass anglers in America in the early 1960s, when Lauri Rapala exported his first black-backed gold

ABOVE
Crankbaits are among the easiest lures for the beginner. They are also top bass producers.

LURES

41

and silver minnows from Finland into the United States. American bass proved to be just as eager to snatch up these first stick minnows as were Finland's pike.

A few inventive fishermen on this side of the Atlantic had already been carving similar minnow imitations, but they had not been used by the general bass-fishing community until Rapala introduced them.

These Rapala lures are widely available to all anglers today and nearly every lure manufacturer produces stick minnow versions.

In the water, very few lures imitate an injured minnow better than the stick minnow, with its mournful side-to-side wobble. The light balsa wood or hollow plastic lure also lands on the water's surface with a delicate plop that offers little threat to any bass nearby.

Although the stick minnow performs well in water, it is among the most difficult lures to cast accurately. A light-action spinning rod and line under 12-pound-test probably give the best results.

Cast the lure well past the target spot and retrieve it through the expected field of vision of the fish. Let it float and bob for a few seconds after landing on the water. Retrieve it (more slowly on bright,

sun-filled days) with an occasional flick of the rod tip to create a spurting, darting action. Every few turns of the reel, stop and allow the lure to float almost back to the surface, then begin the retrieve again. This method most closely approximates the actions of a live, but injured minnow.

FLIES AND TOPWATER LURES

Minnow imitation is also crucial to anglers who pursue bass with fly rods. New patterns of fur and feather are emerging each year. Some are known nationwide; others have more local reputations and names.

The important thing is to match the type and action of the minnow that inhabits the place where

ABOVE

The classic stick minnow remains effective on bass and many other species of gamefish.

≈

RIGHT

Streamers, poppers and bassbugs imitate everything from minnows, frogs and insects to mice.

≈

you are fishing. Sculpin minnows, for example, are a widespread family of about 111 species that tend to stay on the bottom in the riffles. The fly imitation must repeat this action, as well as matching the coloration of the local population. It must bump the bottom to be effective.

Minnows are only one variety of the flies available for bass. Poppers, mimic frogs, small rodents and an array of top-water insects, and cork- and hair-bodied bugs are also available. Long, undulating streamers of rabbit fur give the underwater appearance of eels or leaches. Innovative crayfish and grasshopper patterns have been developed. And bass are not above feeding on larger versions of the same dry fly patterns that trout anglers have been using for years.

More widely used than the bassbugs, but working the same general region of the water, are the topwater lures, including propeller, chugger and popper plugs. The object of these lures is to create a commotion on the surface of the water that mimics some creature swimming or struggling there. Famous members of this family of lures include the Jitterbug, Flatfish and Hula Popper, now available in an assortment of sizes and designs.

Floating/diving lures are excellent for spring bass fishing, when the fish have moved into the shallows. Even with the slower retrieve that the fish require at this sluggish time of the year, many of these lures can get down to bounce along the bottom.

Buzzbaits look more like underwater spinners than topwater lures, but they are actually designed to be retrieved across the surface at a fast clip, their huge forward blades sending up a spray of water. The buzzbait allows an angler to cover the water a great deal more quickly than many other lures.

Topwater fishing with any of these lures and flies is an exciting way to take bass. The strikes are on the surface and are quite explosive.

SINKING LURES

At the other end of the spectrum are the lures which sink under their own weight after hitting the water. Many are designed to drop through the water at a specific rate, allowing the angler to count down until the lure has fallen to the depth that he wants to fish. In addition, many of these lures are equipped with oversized lips, like those on crankbaits, that help to achieve even greater depths and more varied actions.

SPINNERBAITS

You could seine-net an entire lake and turn over every rock without finding anything alive that looks like a spinnerbait, until you consider the flashing, vibrating motion of the blade or blades. There, in the turning blade, is the flashing side of an injured minnow, a favorite easy meal for the bass. Alternatively, the blade may lead the bass to strike simply through its action.

Blades are of three basic designs: teardrop, pear-shaped and willow-leaf. They are attached as single blades or in tandem pairs. Teardrop blades generate the greatest vibration, while the more streamlined willow-leaf designs generate the least. Tandem arrangements produce more vibration than single blades.

This variety allows the spinnerbaits to be used throughout the year, without sacrificing their famous slower retrieve. Matching the current conditions is, as always, of the utmost importance. For example, the larger baitfish produce more vibration in late summer than they do during their much smaller stage in the early spring.

Likewise, summer bass, living in sun-warmed waters, expect faster movements in the baitfish, which means quicker retrieval of the spinnerbait but without too much vibration. Different designs of spinnerbaits will accommodate all these conditions and more.

There are clearly more options with the spinnerbait than the straight retrieve of this versatile lure. Jigging up and down along the edge of some bass cover is now a possibility. The blade action is still there. Bouncing the lure along a rocky bottom is also now feasible.

Spinnerbaits should be brought through the tangles and snags as often as around them in order to attract bass. Gently bounce them off submerged logs and give them a second or two to fall on the near side after the bounce. The design of these lures generally will prevent them from snagging the log.

Many spinnerbaits come equipped with rubber or plastic, which, while they can help attract the bass, should be seen as optional extras. Pork rind, plastic worms or grubs, nightcrawlers, and minnows all might prove more productive under different situations.

Color is the least important of all the lure's aspects. Unpainted metal is probably as effective as any color, but who wants to use something that plain when it doesn't matter anyway?

BELOW

A jig will take bass anywhere, if the jig offers an action that the bass has seen in its natural world.

≈

OTHER LURES

Spoons and spinners work the same region of the water as the spinnerbaits. While spoons produce best results when worked in a slow, fluttering motion, spinners can generate success in a variety of actions, so long as the spinner blade is turning. Both seek to imitate the swimming actions of a baitfish.

Vibrating lures have featured in bass fishing for more than two decades, but only recently have the "rattlers" become a major part of the sport. The rattle that the BBs set up inside the hollow of the lures as they wobble through the water imitates the sounds given off by an injured minnow.

LEFT

Spinners can be effective against bass, particularly in the "whitewater" of streams and rivers.

BELOW

Vibrating lures are equipped with BBs inside their hollow body cavities that produce sounds intended to mimic wounded minnows.

They are available in shapes ranging from flat, pointy shad imitations to sleek minnows, similar to the stick minnows, and in floating and sinking models. The shad shapes wiggle more as they are retrieved and thus rattle the most.

Simple crankbait-type retrieves, the lift-drop jigging action employed with plastic worms, trolling and downrigging can all produce action with these vibrating lures.

A final tip is sometimes to do the exact opposite of what seems logical. This can be especially true on heavily fished lakes.

If most anglers on a body of water seem to be using similar lures in similar ways and meeting with success, by all means join the crowd. On the other hand, if they are not doing all that well, and are only doing it that way because "that's the way it's done, always has been", maybe you should break away from the crowd.

If stick minnows have always been the most productive in the past but have started performing less well, perhaps you want to try plastic worms. If most anglers here are off the water at night, and are no longer getting good results, get out there at night.

Fly fishing is a method that most bass will not yet have seen. Offer them a popper or hair-bug and see what happens.

ABOVE

On heavily fished waters, try anything different, no matter how outlandish it may seem.

LOCATING BASS

SIGNS OF BASS

Many spots look as though they should hold bass but, as we all know, by no means all of them do. The real trick when locating bass spots, particularly on unfamiliar waters, is to look for more than one sign that there are bass to be found.

Cover is almost always the first indication of the presence of bass. Beds of lily pads, grasses or other aquatic vegetation; stumps; a deep bend in the river; or a steep drop-off along the stream could each serve as your starting point. Then check out other features of the environment.

What is the bottom like? Does it provide the sandy or pebbly surface that bass prefer? Some of the more sophisticated fish/depth finders on the market today will offer a reading on the bottom. So will the shoreline, which probably continues in a similar fashion under the water. A rocky shoreline generally leads to a rocky bottom.

Likewise, the shoreline can reveal something about the depth of the water. Gradual inclines on the shoreline probably continue into the water, and steep drops are likely to continue steep.

Do you see any baitfish in the immediate vicinity of the cover? Remember that, above all else, bass are predators. They are found where their prey is found Are there schools of minnows darting about? Do you see any of them jumping from the water in an attempt to elude predators? Are large wading birds working through the area? They eat the same baitfish as the bass.

These environmental factors will suggest exactly how good this spot might be. Is it worth a few casts? Would a shallow-running crankbait or a deep-diver make the best of the given conditions?

One further factor that can mark out any bit of cover as a bass-site is uniqueness. Is it the one bunch of weeds that stands slightly apart from the rest? Is there a partially submerged tree growing next to one particular stump? The conditions that make a bit of cover stand out as special often seem to hold extra attraction for bass.

EDGES AND STICK-UPS

Large bass in particular are careful about how much energy they expend for every meal they get. Getting close is not good enough in bass fishing. This can be painfully obvious when working submerged trees and stumps. A lure retrieved past the tree on one side may excite no interest, while the same lure brought past the opposite side will draw the strike.

Understandably, these 'stick-up' areas are the hotspots of late summer and fall, after the weedbeds have begun to deteriorate and lose their holding power for baitfish and bass alike. They often cover large expanses of a lake or reservoir, making the choice of the exact fishing spot something of a gamble. However, a topographic map drawn before

the area was flooded or a lake survey map can narrow the field of possibilities. Look for the things that can create an edge, such as drop-offs or an old stream channel.

The weedbeds that grow in profusion every summer should be fished with enthusiasm. The edges are the real hotspots, where bass will lie in ambush for passing prey. Most anglers think of the exterior edges of a weedbed when we talk of edges, but actually there are many interior edges that also need to be explored with your lures. The large spots of darker water within and among the weedbed, for example, are generally there for a reason. Perhaps a large boulder or rock pile lies on the bottom at that spot or maybe it is a drop-off. Either would hold an attraction for bass.

Fishing weedbeds can mean frustrating snags and line rips, but moving to slightly heavier gear can get round this problem. With a medium-action rod and line-test of more than 12 pounds (5.4kg), it is possible to tug most weed-snags free.

Weedless spoons and weedless topwater lures can also be a godsend under these conditions. To be effective, these lures must skim across the tops of the weeds while generating enough motion to interest a bass. Watch a few frogs work their ways across a weedbed and you'll get the idea.

Each spring, most lakes, streams and rivers offer a cover type that falls somewhere between stick-up and weedbed. The high waters of spring generally flood the brush and shrubs in the low-lying surrounding areas. As the bass move into the shallower waters for spawning, they use these areas as just another form of weedbed. Topwater lures, normally real producers in weedbeds, will seem unnatural this early in the year, but slowly retrieved spinnerbaits will mimic the baitfish that have also gathered in this temporary cover. The spinnerbaits also allow the angler to cover more water area, which is important at this time of the year, when the bass are more mobile and less likely to hold firmly to any given spot.

Plastic worms and grubs are another effective choice in these brushy conditions. They can be fished almost vertical, down into the branches and tangles.

ABOVE LEFT
Read the story that the lake shore has to offer. These three boats are obviously anchored at a steep drop-off.

BELOW LEFT
The shoreline reveals the rocky drop-off under the water for these bass anglers.

TECHNIQUES FOR FISHING EDGES, COVER AND STICK-UPS

FEATURES	LURES TO USE	TACTICS	
Areas of shoreline vegetation flooded by spring rains, eg brush and willow.	Buzzbait or spinnerbait.	Work a buzzbait through grasses or brush where flooding has occurred. Cast the lure past the normal waterline into the flooded area, and retrieve through the newly submerged vegetation.	
Underwater ledges, sunken boulders, submerged caves.	Spinnerbait, crankbait, small jig, plastic worm.	Bass often like rocky undercuts. Try a crankbait rigged to run under the overhang.	
Brush, dead evergreens, large deciduous trees, wooded areas flooded by reservoirs.	Jig, spoon, plastic worm, pork rind, spinnerbait, buzzbait, big topwater lures.	In spring, big bass may be attracted by a spinnerbait cast near a submerged creek channel running through standing timber.	
Stump beds from logging, dead trees from mud slides, deadfalls from standing timber etc.	Pork rind, plastic worm, crankbait, buzz-bait, spinnerbait, topwater plug.	Big bass often head to drift piles and submerged stumps; cast a topwater plug over these structures.	
Free-floating vegetation (duckweed), emergent (rushes), floating (water lily), submergent (coontail, elodea, pondweed), filamentous algae (moss).	Topwater frog, popper, spoon, buzzbait, propeller lure, minnow imitations, plastic worm, pork rind.	Among floating leaves such as lily pads, use a popper that can be twitched in place, cast in a gap between the leaves.	

When you catch a fish in this type of cover, accept it as an omen and look for spots that replicate it. For example, if it is the brush off the points that is holding the fish, get your lures to those spots.

Other edges may be less obvious at first. The area where a stream empties into a lake or reservoir is edge, in that it is the meeting of two distinct environments. Here you will find a mix of the inhabitants of both moving and standing water, and a year-round range of water temperatures. The bass will take advantage of both.

Generally you will need a fish/depth finder to locate rock piles and rock ridges lying in 8 to 20 feet (2.5 to 6.5m) of water, which are often effective bass magnets. More obvious are those rock piles and ridges that reveal their topmost layers through the surface.

In many rivers and streams, mid- to late summer is an optimum time for locating these structures as the water level is at its lowest. Draw yourself a map of the best spots for future reference.

Rocky edges are a draw for all bass species, but the smallmouth seems to need them more than all others. One explanation may be the species' passion for crayfish, which are also found in the greatest numbers in the rocks. Another factor may be the smallmouth's need for extremely gravelly areas for spawning.

Bass will make use of manmade structures such as bridge pilings and pier or dock posts just as they make use of rock piles and natural stick-ups. These may be some of the most underfished waters on your favorite lake or river.

BELOW
A deep, rocky hole with lots of obstructions and many ledges cries out to be fished.

BOTTOM
Manmade structures, such as this one made of old tires, have a strong attraction for predatory fish like bass.

BELOW

*Downrigging is not the
normal method of fishing of
bass . . .*

≈

ABOVE

*. . . but in deeper waters, it
can produce nice results,
like this Lake Erie three-
pounder (1.4kg).*

≈

Deep waters at 30, 40, even 50 feet (10 to 16m) down are often neglected by the average fisherman as too difficult to fish. However, those anglers may be passing up the chance at some truly large bass. As so often, structure is the key.

Topographic maps of manmade lakes and reservoirs will help you to locate the pre-existing stream channels and drop-offs. The chances are that these were not changed when the reservoir was dammed. They will still be down there, holding bass.

Increasingly, large and popular fishing waters are having their structures mapped by enterprising individuals. The maps are advertised through several outdoor magazines and are often sold through local tackle shops. They will prove a handy addition to your fishing equipment.

A fish/depth finder will not only provide a similar, completely up-to-date map of what is below the boat, but will also give a reading on the fish that are holding there. Large marks should obviously be fished to, but don't neglect the schools of baitfish that your graph registers.

RIVERS AND STREAMS

≈

Bass in rivers and streams (meaning smallmouth for much of the continent and spotted for a smaller region) are creatures of the holes in spring, fall and winter, but move into the rapids and riffles as the hot days of summer take hold.

For much of the year, these rivers and streams can be fished with many of the shallow lake techniques and lures discussed earlier. Floating/diving plugs, shallow runners, spinnerbaits, plastic worms, and so on, but not the deep diving lures, will function properly in this environment. Stickups and fallen trees will provide near-surface structure to encourage the use of topwater lures, as will the many weedbeds that spring up in mid- to late spring each year.

During the summer months, live bait and spinners cast into the rapids are hard to beat. The spot where a riffle empties into a deep hole is prime smallmouth holding water. The riffle is marked by white water and the deep hole is marked by dark, relatively calm water. A large obstruction, such as a rock or log, will create smallmouth water on both sides to the downstream side.

Topwater, floating and floating/shallow diving lures can also produce excellent results in these spots. Cast the lure just upstream of the spot and let it drift down in the current. Twitch it a couple of times, let it float a short way further downstream, twitch it a couple more times, let it float a little further downstream, twitch it a couple more times. Continue in this manner until the lure has moved across the surface of the entire spot.

In this type of fishing, you will do well to remember that the bass spend their days watching natural objects moving past them in the current. They know the look of something alive, either traveling with or struggling against the current. Likewise, they know

that rarely have they seen anything moving across the current for any distance.

Approach the riffles from the bottom, first fishing the hole that they empty into, and then moving upstream, fishing each likely holding water as you move. In this way, fish hooked where you started won't telegraph your presence to other potential catches upstream.

When you catch a nice fish in a spot on a river or stream that you might be fishing again in the future, make a firm mental note of the exact spot where

that fish was holding when you hooked it. Optimum holding/feeding locations are often at a premium on rivers and streams, and other fish will quickly occupy a spot that has been vacated. The next fish may even be in residence within a few days.

Most that can be said about fish-holding structure for bass in lakes will also hold true in streams and rivers, so long as you keep two additional factors in mind: the water in a stream or river is constantly moving downstream, and most streams and rivers are quite a bit shallower than lakes.

A point or bar along the stream or river will hold bass. The point where a smaller stream enters the larger body of water can be a gold-mine. Shallow, slow-moving spots, created by bends in the water-way, are favored spawning grounds. Ledges, ridges and undercuts are all prime bass locations, and are common throughout most streams and rivers.

SEASONAL WATER LAYERING

ABOVE

What is the best time to fish? Whenever you can steal away for even a few casts.

≈

E = *epilimnion (warm waters at the surface)*
T = *thermocline (where temperatures drop quickly from the warm surface to the colder depths)*
H = *hypolimnion (cold, newly oxygenated waters at lake bottom)*

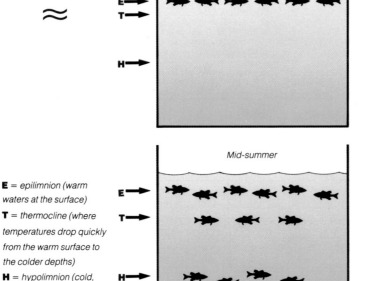

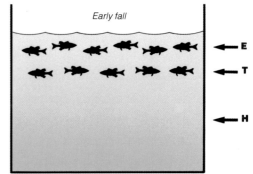

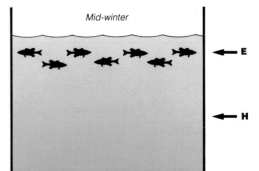

As water layering undergoes seasonal variations, fish-holding areas also change according to the seasons.

THE SEASONS

Fall has long been viewed as a prime time of the year by bass enthusiasts. As the waters begin to cool off from the summer's heat, the bass begin to move back into shallower water, feeding heavily on the healthy crop of minnows that have fattened there during the summer.

The good fishing will continue through much of the fall, until temperatures start to slide to the low 50° or 60° Fahrenheit (10° or 15° C) level.

Throughout this time of the year, the weedbeds that once filled the shallower areas are gradually dying off. But this doesn't mean that the longer surviving weedbeds have lost their attraction for bass. Instead, it means that there are fewer beds that you need to work with each passing week. Your chances of picking the right ones are getting better.

Brown and other non-green weedbeds at this time of the year are good bets to avoid. Once their green color has vanished, they begin to decompose and now remove oxygen from the water, instead of returning it.

Generally the last weedbeds to disappear completely will be those in the shallowest water. The sunlight still has a daily heating effect here. The dominant, large bass are likely to push their way into these spots to take advantage of the last few green plants.

Summer has never received the accolades of spring or fall as a prime bass season. Sun-drenched, hot water means inactive fish, to many an angler. It is true that bass feeding activity does slow as water temperatures exceed 80° Fahrenheit (28° C), but only a little. This is the time of year when there is the most abundant supply of food, which helps to maintain feeding activity. Hot water sets the fish on the move to more comfortable situations.

PRIME LOCATIONS FOR DAY AND NIGHT FISHING

Hot weather suggestions are marked on this diagram.

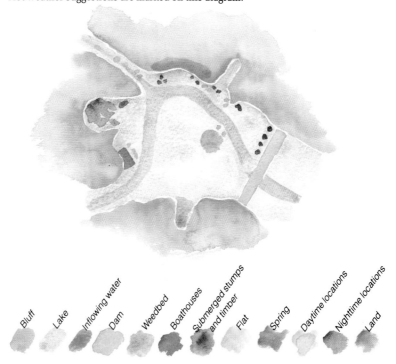

TYPICAL FEATURES OF A SMALL BASS LAKE

LEFT

*Barrel-bodied largemouth
bass may be waiting
among the roots of these
trees in a southern swamp*

Hotter water generally contains less oxygen than cold, so the oxygen-rich weedbeds offer extra attraction as a source of baitfish and other food aplenty at this time of year.

Unless you plan to drop bait through a hole cut in the ice, winter is on the whole the doldrums of bass fishing. However there are two notable exceptions. On many of our rivers today we find electric power plants. In their accompanying warm water discharges, we will find large numbers of bass that remain quite active through what would otherwise be a dormant period. The point where the waters of a spring or small spring-fed stream enter a river can have this same effect, although to a lesser degree because the water is not as warm.

UNFAMILIAR WATERS

New waters offer excitement and challenge, but they also offer many unknown factors, at least at first glance. A good local bass guide, preferably one recommended by former clients, is generally worth much more than the few hundred dollars he will charge to share his knowledge through a day-trip.

Local tackle and bait shops are another reliable source of information about the unfamiliar water. More often than not the owners of these shops are in the business because they earnestly love the sport. Respect their local knowledge and tap into it.

In addition, you can apply everything you have learned on your favorite waters to this new spot. Think about the similarities and use them to your advantage. Match today's conditions and cover types with similar ones that have produced fish in the past. All these methods will enhance your chances of catching fish on new waters.

One final tip is, once in a while, to forget your objections to fishing near cities and towns. Most fishermen justifiably want to escape the hustle and bustle of the modern world so they ignore these waters. But if you try them, you may be pleasantly surprised. For example, the Harrisburg area of the Susquehanna River has proved itself to me in the past as one of the most underfished smallmouth bass locations in the state of Pennsylvania.

AFTER *THE*

CATCH

ABOVE

*Catch-and-release is an
individual decision for each
angler, although a lunker
like this can quickly sway
that choice.*

KEEPING FISH
≈

A major part of my philosophy about bass fishing is the catch-and-release approach to fishing. Release as many of the bass that you hook as possible; give back what you take to the resource and the sport.

This ideal, however, does not preclude keeping a meal or two of fine fat bass every now and again. The bass offers a wonderfully flaky flesh that is second to none when prepared properly.

Preparation should begin the minute you decide to keep a fish. A cooler filled with ice is definitely worth considering when setting out on a fishing trip, if you are planning to keep a meal or so. Immediately kill the fish you intend to keep and place them in the cooler, surrounded by ice. No other technique will keep the flesh fresher for the table.

If using a cooler is not feasible, keep the fish alive in a livewell or on a stringer in the water. Stick the safety-pin-type hook of the stringer through the thin skin behind the lower lip. Do not insert the hook toward the gill cover, or the fish will soon die.

Stream fishermen will want to choose between dragging a stringer in the water with them or killing the fish and carrying them in a wicker or canvas creel. Either method is acceptable if the fish are put on ice within a few hours.

The gills and guts should be removed from killed fish as soon as possible after they are killed, rather than at the end of the day.

FILLETING
≈

While many fish are bonier than bass, most people prefer boneless fillets to a prepared whole fish. Filleting is easier than it looks. Keep the blade of the fillet knife as sharp as possible to make the following steps easier to follow:

BELOW

Filleting fish is not at all difficult, depending largely on the sharpness of your knife.

≈

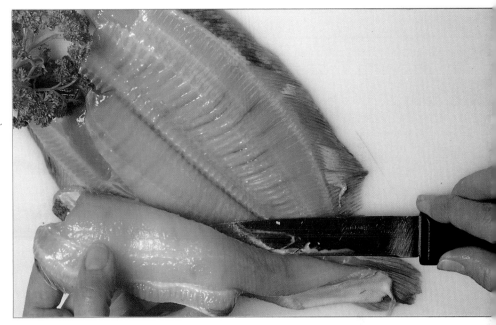

~ Cut twice along the back of the fish, once on each side of the dorsal fin, from head to causal fin. Make the cuts as close to the dorsal fin as possible, and as deep as the backbone.

~ Insert the knife blade flat along the flank and cut the flesh away from the bones on one side, moving from the fish's back to its belly.

~ Repeat step 2 on the other side.

~ Skin the fillets by laying them skin side down on a cutting board. Slide the knife blade between the skin and the flesh, from back to belly and move the blade from the rear of the fillet to its front. Slant the knife blade toward the skin all the while.

RECICES

My brother Bruce, who is both a better angler and a better cook than I, passed on the following recipes. They all do full justice to a bass fillet. I have used and can highly recommend each.

GRILLED BASS AND VEGETABLES

INGREDIENTS:
Bass fillets
Green peppers
Onions
Tomatoes
Grated mozzarella cheese
Dried hot pepper
Herbal salt substitute

Slice the vegetables.

On a large piece of aluminium foil, lay down a layer of pepper slices the size of your bass fillet, then a layer of sliced onion, a layer of sliced tomato and your fillet. Repeat the layers in reverse on the other side of the fillet.

Sprinkle a dash of herbal salt substitute between each layer.

Spread the mozzarella cheese over the top of the whole layered affair, top with a light sprinkle of dried hot pepper and seal the aluminium foil package at all edges.

Place the package on a grill over barbecue coals or an open fire, or in the oven at 350 degrees Fahrenheit (155°C), for about 30 minutes, turning the package once.

The package is cooked thoroughly when the fish flakes at the touch of a fork. Serve with hard Italian bread.

FRESHWATER SHRIMP

INGREDIENTS:
Bass fillets
Bisquick
Ginger ale
Quality cooking oil

Cut the bass fillets into finger-sized strips. Mix a thick batter of Bisquick and ginger ale. Heat the oil on the rangetop until a bit of batter balls up immediately upon being dropped in it.

Dip the bass strips into the batter and then drop them into the oil to deep fry. Remove each one as soon as it is deep fried.

Serve the bass strips with the same sauces that you would use for breaded shrimp.

This method of preparing fish has been adapted for use with walleye and is a favorite at several outfitter lodges in Quebec.

RIGHT
A nice, medium-sized largemouth is perfect for the pan.

PINEAPPLED BASS

INGREDIENTS:

Bass fillets
22-ounce (600g) can of unsweetened, crushed pineapple
2 teaspoons of sugar
1 teaspoon of salt
Garlic powder
Soy sauce
2 tablespoons of quality cooking oil
8–10 green tops of scallions

~ Create a marinade by combining the pineapple, its juice, sugar, salt, and garlic powder and soy sauce to taste.

~ Place the bass fillets in the marinade and let the whole mix stand in the refrigerator for 3–4 hours.

~ Remove the marinaded fillets and place them into a baking dish. Pour the cooking oil over them. Cut the scallion tops, not the lower portion of the scallions that are normally eaten, over the fillets and oil.

~ Bake at 300 degrees Fahrenheit (145°C) for 20–30 minutes, until the flesh flakes at the touch of a fork.

~ Pour the marinade sauce over the fillets and scallion tops, and back for about 30 minutes at 350 degrees Fahrenheit (155°C).

~ This is adapted from a Vietnamese recipe that obviously used fish other than black bass as the principal ingredient, but it makes a magnificent bass dish.

BASS IN ORANGE

INGREDIENTS:

Bass fillets
Bisquick
1 egg
½ cup fresh-squeezed orange juice
1 orange
Margarine

Dip the fillets in the beaten egg and then into the Bisquick to lightly flour them. Fry them in margarine until lightly browned.

Place the fried fillets in a baking dish, dribble the orange juice over them slowly and lay slices of the orange on top of them.

Cover the baking dish and bake for 30 minutes at 300 degrees Fahrenheit (145℃), checking occasionally to determine if the orange juice has cooked away and adding a bit more if it has. Remove the cover for the final 10 minutes of baking.

ABOVE
Shallow frying fish for
Bass in Orange.

THE **FUTURE**

OF THE

SPORT

In years past a stringer at its limit was the measure of success for any fisherman, including one of the bass fraternity. When it seemed that the resource was endlessly renewable, we were all guilty of killing more fish than we needed.

Those innocent days are gone. With over 70 million of us putting pressure on it, the resource needs a hand to renew itself. That hand, which more and more bass anglers are practising, is catch-and-release.

For many anglers today a successful catch is a fish brought to the side of the boat and released before it ever leaves the water. Immediately, the resource has been renewed. That same fish will provide action on another day. It might take part in the next spawn, generating the next generation of bass. This in-water method of release is the one that best insures the survival of the fish.

Netting a fish or letting it bounce about on land or on the bottom of a boat generally removes some of its protective mucous coating, which can lead to infection. Handling the fish totally in the water lessens this problem.

Slender, long-nosed pliers are helpful for the in-water method of release. Many lures, especially barbless and single-hook, can be reversed out of a bass's mouth by pulling them with the pliers.

Deep-hooked fish, often those caught on live bait, will have to be given the hook. Simply snip the line as close to the hook as possible and release the fish. All hooks will eventually corrode, although gold, bronze and blue hooks go through this proces much faster than stainless steel.

Bass are among the easier fish to immobilize. They do not need to be grasped tightly about the midsection, in the eye sockets or under the gill plates. They can be held by the lip while the angler removes the hook, although the angler must be cautious of where the hook is, for his own safety.

Fish that have been played hard and long will

(59cm), 8½ pounds (3.8kg); 24 inches (60cm), just over 9 pounds (4.1kg). As with any generalization such as this, there will be wide variation between individual fish.

Catch-and-release began in trout fishing and spread quickly into other areas of the angling fraternity. It was first realized to be necessary to ensure the future of the resource in the mid-1950s. Two forks of the Little Pigeon River, a trout stream in Great Smoky Mountains National Park, were probably the first officially designated catch-and-release waters. At the time the concept was referred to as fish-for-fun, a name that held up until about the mid-1960s when someone pointed out that most fishing is done for fun.

ABOVE
Even large bass can be immobilized when their lower lips are secured.

need special care for proper release. Swim the fish, just as the fish would swim on its own, to force oxygen-carrying water across its gills. Don't let go of it, until the fish pulls to get away from your grasp.

Fisheries biologists across the country have developed a standard for determining the approximate weight of a largemouth bass from its length. This may be of some use to catch-and-release anglers who want to know what their catch weighed.

A largemouth of 12 inches (30cm) in length will generally weigh about 1 pound (0.45kg); 13¾ inches (34cm), 1½ pounds (0.68kg); 15 inches (37.5cm), 2 pounds (0.9kg); 16¼ inches (40.5cm), 2½ pounds (1.14kg); 17 inches (42.5cm), 3 pounds (1.36kg); 17¾ to 18 inches (45cm), 3½ pounds (1.58kg); 18¾ inches (46.9cm), 4 pounds (1.82kg); 19¼ inches (48cm), 4½ pounds (2kg); 20 inches (50cm), 5 pounds (2.3kg); 20½ inches (51cm), 5½ pounds (2.49kg); 21 to 21¼ inches (53cm), 6 pounds (2.72kg); 21¾ inches (54cm), 6½ pounds (2.94kg); 22¼ inches (56cm), 7 pounds (3.2kg); 22½ to 22¾ inches (57cm), 7½ pounds (3.42kg); 23 to 23¼ inches (58cm), 8 pounds (3.6kg); 23¾ inches

RIGHT
If possible, keep a bass in the water at all times before releasing it. This minimizes trauma and injury to the fish.

The Little Pigeon River experiment proved successful, dramatically improving both the catch rate and the size of the trout being caught. Other waters in other parts of the country were gradually brought under similar restrictions.

Catch-and-release works. It's that simple, and it's been proven many times through scientific studies.

State fish and game agencies have required a certain measure of catch-and-release for many years through seasons, bag limits and minimum size restrictions. More recently, some agencies have refined this concept by also placing a maximum size limit and a slot size limit on fish to be kept.

However, not all the fish can or should be released. Bleeders, especially those with hooks about the gills, have a reduced chance of survival. Obviously diseased fish should be culled from the population, although these should not be used for the table.

For the angler wanting a meal of bass, which is an honest and worthy desire, the smaller, legal fish will provide the best table fare. Release the larger ones to maintain the level of the sport. Many hostile factors make it difficult for truly large fish to reach that size. Why not re-use such a prize again and again?

The closing words of James Henshall in his first-ever book on bass fishing seem appropriate at this point:

". . . AND EVER BE SATISFIED WITH A MODERATE CREEL.

"By so doing, your angling days will be happy, and your sleep undisturbed; and you, and I, and the fish we may catch, can say, with the sweet singer of Israel:

"'The lines are fallen to me in pleasant places.'"

ABOVE

Pressure is increasing on our bass waters at a phenomenal rate. Perhaps stringers like this one will soon be relegated to the history of the sport.

RIGHT

Research is under way by fish and game agencies to determine the impact of heavy fishing. Here a largemouth is fitted with a tracking tag.

HOTSPOTS

To compile this section of the book I asked fish and game agencies across the continent to supply information about bass fishing within their States and Provinces. Some were quick to send an abundance of information, others were not. For the latter, we have used information from other sources.

This listing should be viewed as nothing more than a starting point for your own explorations of bass waters. (The imperial measurements are exactly as supplied; the metric equivalents are approximate.)

ALABAMA

The State record largemouth was taken from Mountain View Lake in 1987. It weighed 16 pounds, 8 ounces (7.5kg). Its smallmouth counterpart was caught in the tailwater at Wheeler Dam in 1950. This former world-record fish weighed in at 10 pounds, 8 ounces (4.8kg). The state record spotted bass came from Lewis Smith Reservoir in 1978, weighing 8 pounds, 15 ounces (4kg).

Recommended top bass waters in this state, according to the Alabama Department of Conservation and Natural Resources, include: Washington County Lake; Guntersville, Wheeler, Wilson and Pickwick reservoirs on the Tennessee River; Lay, Neely Henry and Logan Martin lakes on the Coosa River; West Point Reservoir; Harris Reservoir; Lewis Smith Lake; Lake Tuscaloosa; Lake Jordan; Lake Harding; Lake Eufala; Lake Jackson; Miller's Ferry; the Mobile Delta; Aliceville Lake; Gainesville Lake; Wilson Lake; Martin Lake.

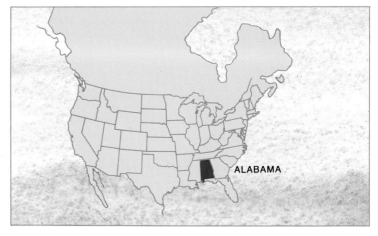

ALABAMA

ARKANSAS

~

The 1984 and 1985 BASS Masters Classic tournament of the Bass Anglers Sportsmen's Society (BASS) were held in Pine Bluff on the Arkansas River, speaking well of the fishery there.

State records are a 16-pound, 4-ounce (7.37kg) largemouth taken from Lake Mallard in 1976; a 7-pound, 15-ounce (3.6kg) spotted bass from Lake Bull Shoals in 1983; and a 7-pound, 5-ounce (3.3kg) smallmouth from Lake Bull Shoals in 1969.

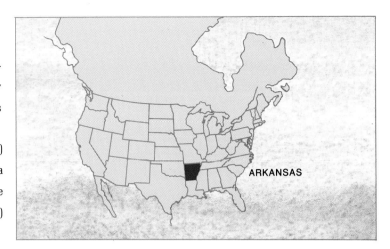

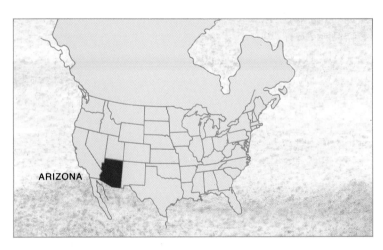

ARIZONA

~

Largemouth bass were introduced into the State in 1897; smallmouth bass in 1921. Today they are the second and third most sought-after fish in the State, after trout, according to a survey of more than 7,500 Arizona anglers conducted by the Arizona Game and Fish Department.

While the huge reservoirs of the Colorado River were the favorites of non-residents, local anglers concentrated nearly as much on the large inland reservoirs, such as Roosevelt, Apache and Bartlett.

The State records are: largemouth, 14 pounds, 8 ounces (6.5kg), taken in 1988 from Roosevelt Lake; and smallmouth, 7 pounds, 10 ounces (3.46kg), taken in 1988 from the same lake.

CALIFORNIA

~

The State record largemouth was taken from Lake Casitas in 1980; it weighed 21 pounds, 3¼ ounces (9.6kg). Its smallmouth and spotted counterparts each weighed 9 pounds, 1 ounce (4.13kg); the record smallmouth was taken from Clair Engle Lake in 1976 and the record spotted bass from Lake Perris in 1984.

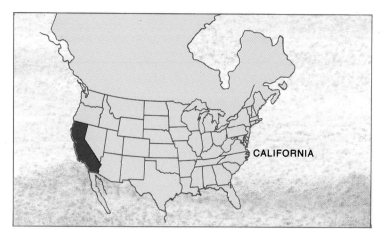

COLORADO

~

State records are a 10 pound, 6¼-ounce (4.7kg) largemouth caught in 1979 in Stalker Lake; and a 5-pound, 8-ounce (2.5kg) smallmouth in 1987 in Pueblo Reservoir.

CONNECTICUT

~

The State record largemouth was taken in 1961 from Mashapaug Lake; it weighed 12 pounds, 14 ounces (5.8kg). Its smallmouth counterpart was caught in 1980 in Shenipsit Lake, weighing 7 pounds, 12 ounces (3.5kg).

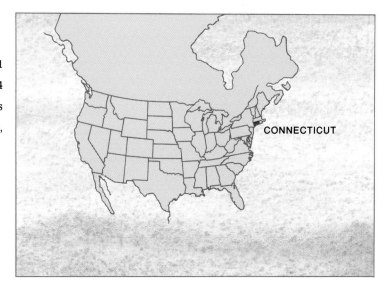

DELAWARE

~

State records are a 10-pound, 5-ounce (4.7kg) large-mouth in Andrews Lake in 1980, and a 4-pound, 7-ounce (2kg) smallmouth in Quarry Pond in 1983.

FLORIDA

~

The 1989 angler surveys by the Florida Game and Fresh Water Fish Commission revealed that the best overall fishing for largemouth bass in the State was to be had on the St John's River in Lake Dexter and upriver, where anglers hooked up with bass at the rate of 0.64 per hour. A similar catch rate was recorded between December 1988 and May 1989 in the Everglades. Other impressive catch rates on keepers (more than 0.33 bass per hour) were noted on world-reknowned Okeechobee, Kissimmee, Harris and Orange lakes.

The State record largemouth of 20 pounds, 2 ounces (9.14kg) was caught in 1923 on appropriately named Big Fish Lake. Its spotted counterpart is a 3-pound, 12-ounce (1.7kg) fish that came from the Apalachicola River in 1985. The Suwannee bass record was set in 1985 by a 3-pound, 14¼-ounce (1.76kg) fish from the Suwannee River.

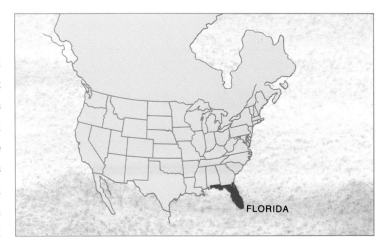

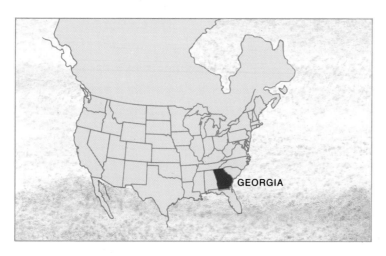

GEORGIA

The current world record (all-tackle) largemouth and Suwannee bass have both come from Georgia. The 22-pound, 4-ounce (10.1kg) largemouth was taken by George Perry in 1932 in Montgomery Lake. That fish also stands as the State's record.

The Suwannee record was a 3-pound, 9-ounce (1.6kg) bass caught by Laverne Norton in 1984 on the Ochlockonee River.

Their counterparts are an 8-pound, ½-ounce (3.6kg) spotted bass in 1985 in Lake Lanier, and a 7-pound, 2-ounce (3.26kg) smallmouth in 1973 in Lake Chatuge.

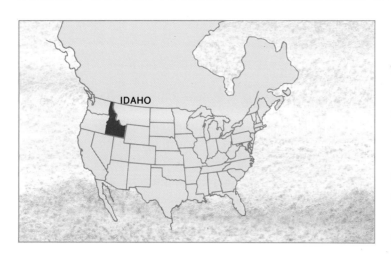

IDAHO

The State record largemouth, 10 pounds, 15 ounces (4.96kg), was taken in Anderson Lake. The State record smallmouth, 7 pound, 5½ ounces (3.36kg), was caught in Dworshak Reservoir.

The Idaho Department of Fish and Game also recommends lakes through the northern part of the State and reservoirs throughout the southwest. For smallmouth, the department points to the Snake and Clearwater rivers and the reservoirs there, as well as Brownlee and Dworshak reservoirs.

ILLINOIS

~

The State record largemouth bass, a 13-pound,
1-ounce (5.93kg) lunker, was pulled from Stone
Quarry Lake in 1976. The State record spotted bass
was caught in a strip-mine in Fulton County in
1982; it weighed 6 pounds, 12 ounces (3kg). And,
the State record smallmouth is a 6-pound, 7-ounce
(2.92kg) fish that was caught in 1985 in a strip-mine
in Fulton County.

The Illinois Department of Conservation offers
these lakes for largemouth: Baldwin, Banner Marsh-
Johnson, Carlinville, Cedar, Channel-Catherine,
Clinton, Coffeen, Dolan, East Fork, Fox, Gillespie
New City, Glenn Shoals, Grass, Greenville New
City, Homer, Horseshoe, Illinois Department of
Transportation, Carlton, Centralia, Egypt, George,
Lou Yeager, Marie, Mingo, Springfield, La Salle,
Lincoln Trail, Long, Mermet, Mill Creek, Newton
CIPS, Paris East, Pierece, Raccoon, Rend, Sam Parr,
Sangchris, Shabbona, Spring, Washington County,
Weldon Springs, Wolf and Waverly.

The department suggests the following waters for
smallmouth: Fox River, Heidecke Lake, Iroquois
River, Kankakee River, Kishwaukee River, Kyte
River, La Salle Lake, Mackinaw River, Middle Fork
Vermilion River, Randolph County Lake, Rock
River, Sterling Lake and Sugar River.

RIGHT
*A warm, foggy morning,
and waters filled with bass
are the stuff of lifetime
memories.*

INDIANA

~

Lake Monroe, a perennial supplier of lunker large-mouth, is a favorite among Hoosier bass anglers, for good reason.

The State record largemouth for Indiana, weighing 11 pounds, 11 ounces (5.3kg), was taken from Ferdinand Reservoir in 1968. The State record smallmouth of 6 pounds, 15 ounces (3.14kg) was caught in Sugar Creek in 1985. And, the State record spotted bass was taken in a small lake in Howard County in 1975; it weighed 5 pounds, 1½ ounces (2.3kg).

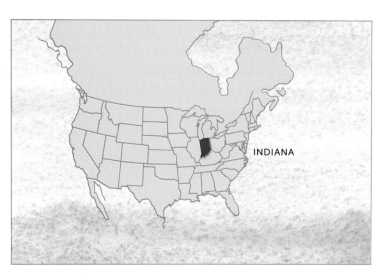

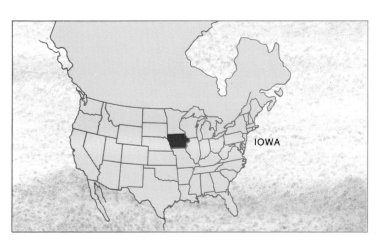

IOWA

~

The State record largemouth of 10 pounds, 12 ounces (4.9kg) was caught in Lake Fisher in May 1984. The State record smallmouth was taken in Spirit Lake in May 1979; it weighed 6 pounds, 8 ounces (2.9kg).

KANSAS

~

The Kansas Fish and Game Commission rates the following waters as excellent for largemouth: Lone Star Lake, El Dorado Reservoir, Harvey County East Lake, Moline City Lake, the Emporia low-water dam on the Cottonwood River, Rooks State Fishing Lake, Logan City Lake. Excellent for spotted bass are: Marion County Lake, Winfield City Lake. Good for small-mouth: Milford Reservoir, Wilson Reservoir, Council Grove City Lake, El Dorado Reservoir.

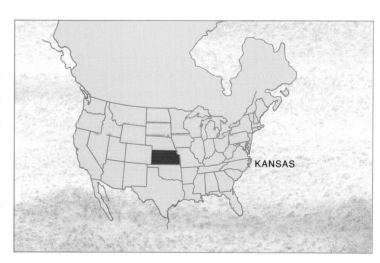

KENTUCKY

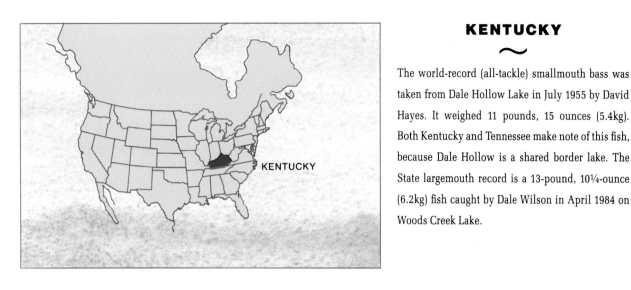

The world-record (all-tackle) smallmouth bass was taken from Dale Hollow Lake in July 1955 by David Hayes. It weighed 11 pounds, 15 ounces (5.4kg). Both Kentucky and Tennessee make note of this fish, because Dale Hollow is a shared border lake. The State largemouth record is a 13-pound, 10¼-ounce (6.2kg) fish caught by Dale Wilson in April 1984 on Woods Creek Lake.

LOUISIANA

The State record largemouth was taken from a farm pond in 1975. It weighed 12 pounds (5.45kg). A 4-pound, 14-ounce (2.2kg) spotted bass holds the record for its species. It was caught in 1976 in the Tickflaw River.

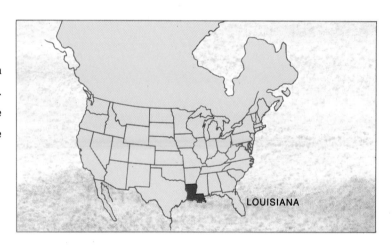

MAINE

State records are an 11-pound, 10-ounce (5.3kg) largemouth on Moose Pond in 1968 and an 8-pound (3.6kg) smallmouth on Thompson Lake in 1970.

MARYLAND

~

The State is noted for the fantastic bass fishing provided by the scattered farm ponds throughout its rural areas, but particularly on the Eastern Shore. In addition, the Maryland Department of Natural Resources manages some waters, such as Deep Creek Lake, with effective trophy bass regulations.

State records are an 11-pound, 2-ounce (5.06kg) largemouth caught in a farm pond in 1983 and an 8-pound, 4-ounce (3.7kg) smallmouth taken from Liberty Reservoir in 1975.

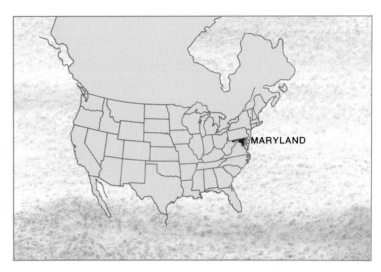

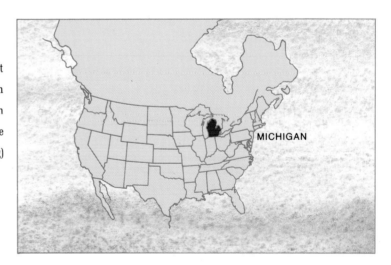

MASSACHUSETTS

~

A 15-pound, 8-ounce (7.02kg) largemouth taken in Sampson's Pond in 1975 holds the State record. Its smallmouth counterpart is a 7-pound, 4-ounce (3.3kg) fish taken from the Quaboag River in 1984.

MICHIGAN

~

State records are tied in the largemouth category at 11 pounds, 15 ounces (5.42kg) between a fish taken in 1934 in Big Pine Island Lake and another taken in 1959 in Bamfield Dam. The uncontested State smallmouth record is a 9-pound, 4-ounce (4.2kg) fish caught in Long Lake in 1906.

LEFT

Farm ponds produce many of the top bass that are caught in Maryland.

≈

MINNESOTA

~

The State record largemouth is an 8-pound, 9½-ounce (3.9kg) lunker pulled from Fountain Lake in 1986. The smallmouth record for the State is held by an 8-pound (3.6kg) fish caught in West Battle Lake in 1948.

MISSISSIPPI

~

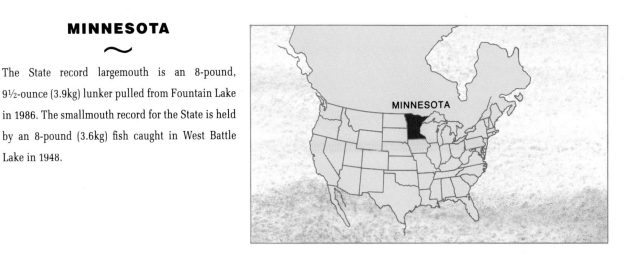

The State record largemouth bass was taken May 3, 1987, in Tippah County Lake. It weighed 14 pounds, 12 ounces (6.7kg). The largest recorded smallmouth was taken January 24, 1987, in Pickwick Reservoir, weighing 7 pounds, 15 ounces (3.6kg). And the State record spotted bass of 8 pounds, 2 ounces (3.66kg) was taken September 2, 1975, from a stream in Jones County.

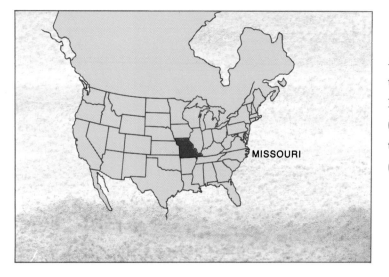

MISSOURI

~

A 13-pound, 14-ounce (6.3kg) largemouth bass holds the State record, taken in 1961 from Bull Shoals Lake. The smallmouth State record is a 7-pounder (3.2kg) caught in 1988 in Stockton Lake. Their spotted bass counterpart weighed 7 pounds, 8 ounces (3.42kg) and was taken in 1966 in Table Rock Lake.

MONTANA

~

The State record largemouth stands at 8 pounds, 2½ ounces (3.66kg), caught in 1984 in Milnor Lake. The smallmouth State record was caught in 1987 in Fort Peck Lake; it weighed 5 pounds (2.27kg).

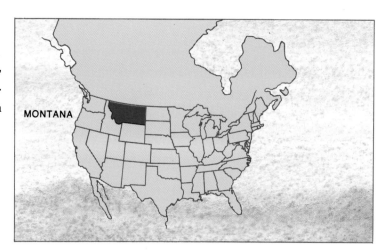

NEBRASKA

~

The 1990 Fishing Forecast from the Nebraska Game and Parks Commission pointed to these waters: Smith Lake, Lake Winters Creek, Island Lake, Pelican Lake, Dewey Lake, West Long, Missouri River, Lewis and Clark Lake.

A 10-pound, 11-ounce (4.85kg) largemouth set the State record in 1965, taken from a sandpit. The State record smallmouth is a 6-pound, 1½-ounce (2.75kg) fish caught in 1978 in Merrit Reservoir.

NEVADA

~

A 1988 survey revealed that fishermen in Nevada spent more than 85 per cent of their time on only 20 of the State's 744 fishable waters. The top 20 were Lake Mead, Lake Mohave, Truckee River, Pyramid Lake, Ruby Marsh, Topaz Reservoir, Eagle Valley Reservoir, Cave Lake, Walker River, Walker Lake, Lake Tahoe, Colorado River, Rye Patch Reservoir, Lahontan Reservoir, Washoe Lake, Echo Canyon Reservoir, Wilson Reservoir, Wildhorse Reservoir, Carson River and Humboldt River.

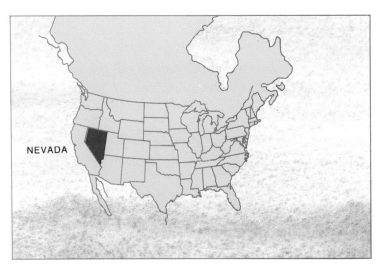

NEVADA

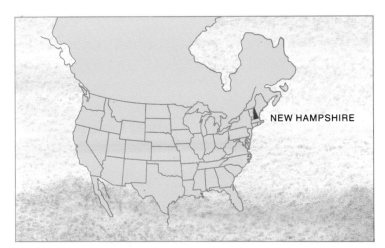

NEW HAMPSHIRE

NEW HAMPSHIRE

~

State records are a 10-pound, 8-ounce (4.76kg) largemouth in 1967 in Lake Pontanipo and a 7-pound, 14½-ounce (3.6kg) smallmouth in 1970 in Goose Pond.

RIGHT
Wherever you find structure like this, cast your lure.

NEW JERSEY

~

A 1989 cooperative study between the New Jersey Division of Fish, Game and Wildlife and the New Jersey BASS Chapter Federation in 18 top bass waters in the State developed the following ranking (in terms of angler success per hour fished) for those waters: Carnegie Lake, Echo Lake, Farrington Lake, Pompton Lake, Budd Lake, Musconetcong Lake, Swartswood Lake, Canistear Lake, Cranbury Lake, Hopatcong Lake, Greenwood Lake, Wawayanda Lake, Delaware River, Maurice Lake, Assunpink Lake, Stone Tavern Lake, Mercer Lake, Deal Lake.

State records stand at 10 pounds, 14 ounces (4.93kg) for largemouth (Menantico Pond, 1980) and 6 pounds, 4 ounces (2.83kg) for smallmouth (the Delaware River, 1957).

NEW MEXICO

~

The State record largemouth is 12 pounds, 8 ounces (5.67kg), caught in 1988 in Bill Evans Lake; smallmouth, 6 pounds, 8¾ ounces (2.95kg), Ute Lake, 1972; and spotted bass, 4 pounds, 8 ounces (2.04kg), Cochiti Lake, 1988.

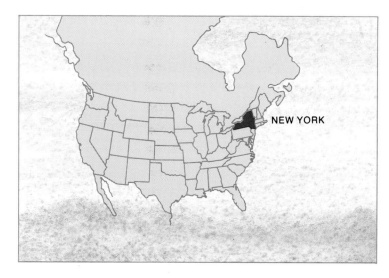

NEW YORK

The St Lawrence River is among the best bass waters across the North American continent, and limit catches of 2- to 4-pound (1 to 2kg) smallmouths and 3- to 5-pound (1.4 to 2.3kg) largemouths are not uncommon.

Other favourite bass waters in this State, according to the New York Division of Fish and Wildlife, include Lake Champlain, Lake George, Long Lake, the Saranac Lakes, Lake Erie, Conesus Lake, Seneca Lake, Niagara River, Lake Ontario, Oneida Lake, Chautauqua Lake.

State records are as follows: largemouth, 11 pounds, 5 ounces (5.14kg), 1987, Buckhorn Lake; smallmouth, 9 pound (4.1kg), 1925, in a small lake (further details unknown).

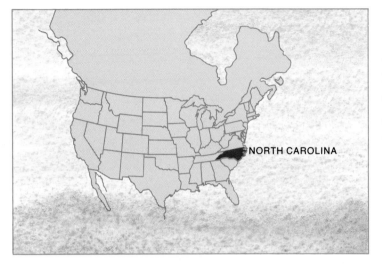

NORTH CAROLINA

~

Some bass recommendations from the North Caro-
lina Wildlife Resources Commission are Lake Mat-
tamuskeet, Lake Phelps, Lake Waccamaw, Tranter's
Creek, Batchler's Creek, Black River, Cashie River,
Yeopin River, Chowan River, Perquiman's Creek,
Pembroke Creek, Tar River (home of the little-known
Roanoke bass), Cape Fear River, Yadkin River, Kerr
Reservoir, Gaston Reservoir, Falls-of-the-Neuse
Lake.

Records: Largemouth, 14 pounds, 15 ounces
(6.78kg), 1963, Santeetlah Reservoir; smallmouth,
10 pounds, 2 ounces (4.6kg), 1953, Hiwassee Reservoir; spotted, 4 pounds, 8 ounces (2.04kg), 1988,
Lake Cahtuge; Roanoke, 2 pounds, 8 ounces (1.14kg),
1978, Hope Mills Lake.

NORTH DAKOTA

~

The State records were set by an 8-pound, 7½-ounce
(3.8kg) largemouth in 1983 in Nelson Lake and a
5-pound, 1-ounce (2.3kg) smallmouth in 1987 in
Lake Sakakawea.

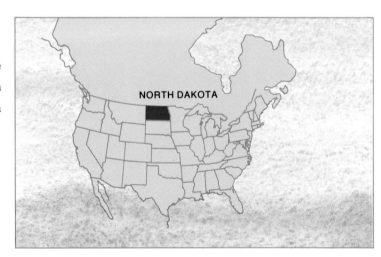

OHIO

~

The State record largemouth, a 13-pound, 2-ounce (5.96kg) fish, was taken from a farm pond in May 1976. The 7-pound, 8-ounce (3.42kg) State record smallmouth was caught in the Mad River in June 1941. The State record spotted bass was taken in Lake White in May 1976; it weighed 5 pounds, 4 ounces (2.38kg).

Highly rated bass waters in the Ohio Department of Natural Resources' 1990 Prospects report included Buckeye Lake, Delaware Lake, Griggs Lake, Indian Lake, Kiser Lake, Knox Lake, O'Shaughnessy Reservoir, Rush Creek Lake.

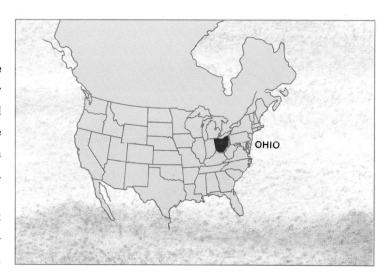

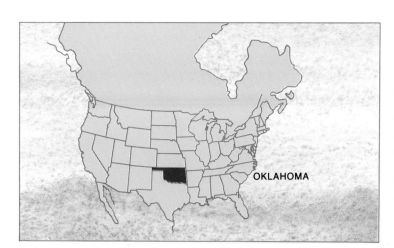

OKLAHOMA

~

The State record largemouth was taken in 1989 in Lake Fuqua; it weighed 12 pounds, 13 ounces (5.8kg). The State record smallmouth is a 6-pound, 7-ounce lunker caught in Lake Texoma in 1989. Their spotted bass counterpart was pulled from a Pittsburg Company pond in 1958; it weighed 8 pounds 2 ounces (3.66kg).

OREGON

~

State records are 11 pounds, 4 ounces (5.11kg) by a largemouth caught in 1988 in Lost Creek Lake and 6 pounds, 14 ounces (3.1kg) by a smallmouth taken in 1989 in the Columbia River.

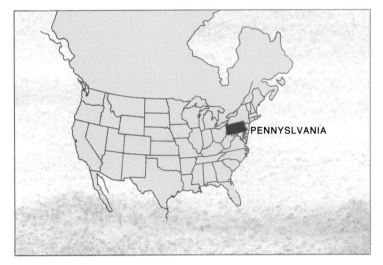

PENNSYLVANIA
~

The Susquehanna River, which transects the State, north to south, through its midsection is among the very best smallmouth fisheries in the East. A tributary, the Juniata River, also offers an extremely healthy population of the fish.

However, the State records are held by a largemouth of 11 pounds, 3 ounces (5.08kg) that came from Birch Run Reservoir in 1983 and a smallmouth of 7 pounds, 5½ ounces (3.35kg) that was taken from the Youghiogheny River in 1983.

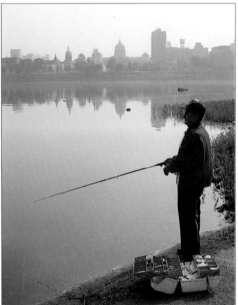

LEFT
The Susquehanna River,
Pennsylvania, and many of
its tributaries, including the
Juniata River and Pine
Creek, are prime
smallmouth bass waters.

ABOVE
In the shadow of
Pennsylvania State's
capital buildings, the
Susquehanna River offers
some of the best bass
water in the East.

RHODE ISLAND

~

State records are 10 pounds, 5 ounces (4.68kg) for largemouth (Wordens Pond, 1987) and 5 pounds, 15 ounces (2.69kg) for smallmouth (Wash Pond, 1977).

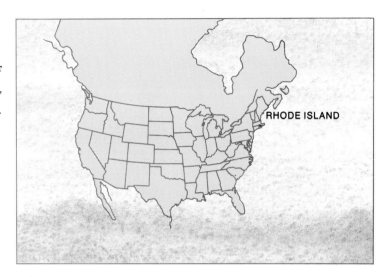

RHODE ISLAND

SOUTH CAROLINA

~

The lakes of the Santee Cooper region are world-famous for their largemouth bass. Lake Marion and Lake Moultrie are top choices. Other lakes that the South Carolina Wildlife and Marine Resources Department rated highly were Hartwell, Russell, Jocassee, Keowee, Thurmond, Wateree and Greenwood.

State records are a 16-pound, 2-ounce (7.12kg) largemouth taken in Lake Marion in 1949; a 6-pound, 12-ounce (3.06kg) smallmouth taken in the Broad River in 1988; and a 4-pound, 7-ounce (2.02kg) spotted bass taken in Lake Hartwell in 1989.

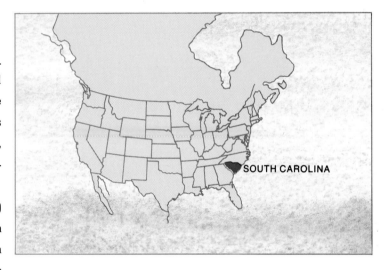

SOUTH CAROLINA

SOUTH DAKOTA

~

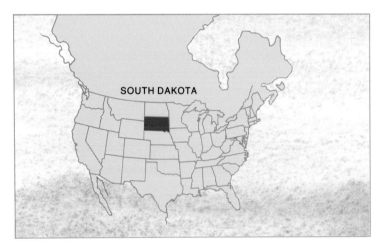

The South Dakota Game, Fish and Parks Department notes Lake Lewis and Clark, as well as farm ponds throughout the eastern part of the State and stock dams in the west, as top bass waters within the State.

The State record largemouth was taken in 1986 in a stock dam in Jackson County; it weighed 8 pounds, 14 pounds (3.99kg). The State record smallmouth came from Clear Lake in 1988; it weighed 5 pounds, 3¼ ounces (2.36kg).

*An angler plies a typical bit
of Tennessee bass water.*

TENNESSEE

The world record (all-tackle) smallmouth bass was taken from Dale Hollow Lake in July 1955 by David Hayes. It weighed 11 pounds, 15 ounces (5.42kg). Both Kentucky and Tennessee make note of this fish, because Dale Hollow is a shared border lake.

According to the Department of Tennessee Wildlife Resources, the average largemouth bass caught in Kentucky Lake weighs nearly two pounds (0.9kg). The State record largemouth was taken from Sugar Creek. It weighed 14 pounds, 8 ounces (6.58kg).

One of the best areas in the State for spotted bass is the Pickwick Tailwater near Savannah. The State record, however, was taken from Center Hill Reservoir. It weighed 5 pounds, 8 ounces (2.49kg).

Other lakes pointed out by the Department for bass include Humboldt, Graham, Maples Creek, Garrett, Whiteville, Barkley, Cheatham, Percy Priest, Old Hickory, Cordell Hull, Woods, Tims Ford, Normandy, Marrowbone, Bedford, Laurel Hill, Center Hill, Watts Bar, Nickajack, Tellico, Fort Loudoun, Melton Hill, Norris, Cherokee, Douglas, Boone-Fort Patrick Henry, South Holston-Watauga.

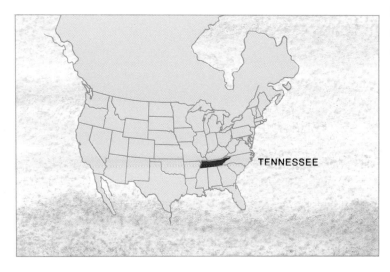

TENNESSEE

TEXAS

A 17-pound, 11-ounce (8.03kg) largemouth set the State record in 1986, taken in Lake Fork. The State record smallmouth was caught in 1988 in Lake Whitney; it weighed 7 pounds, 11½ ounces (3.51kg). A spotted bass weighing 5 pounds, 9 ounces (2.52kg), taken in 1966 in Lake O' the Pines, holds the record for that species. And a 3-pound, 11-ounce (1.67kg) Guadalupe bass established that species' record in 1983 on Lake Travis.

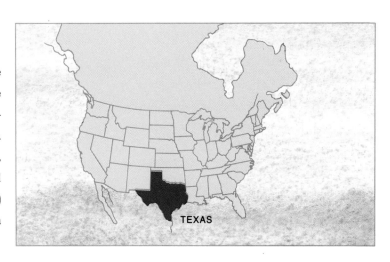

TEXAS

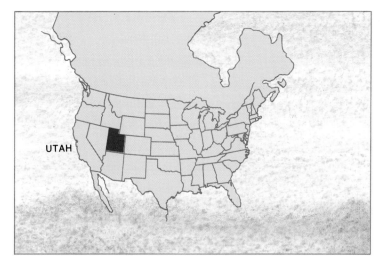

UTAH

~

According to the Utah Division of Wildlife Resources, the following waters are the State's primary largemouth fisheries: Lake Powell, Gunlock Reservoir, Huntington North Reservoir, Red Fleet Reservoir, Pineview Reservoir, Pelican Lake. Waters with fishable smallmouth populations are Lake Powell, Flaming Gorge Reservoir, Rockport Reservoir, Starvation Reservoir, Piute Reservoir, Newcastle Reservoir.

Of the division's list of the State's top 20 fishing spots are the following bass waters: Deer Creek Reservoir, Flaming Gorge Reservoir, Lake Powell, Piute Reservoir, Utah Lake.

State records: largemouth, 11 pounds, 2 ounces (5.06kg), 1974, Lake Powell; smallmouth, 6 pounds, 12 ounces (3.06kg), 1983, Lake Borham.

VERMONT

~

The State record largemouth was recorded in the Connecticut River in 1986, at 9 pounds, 11 ounces (4.4kg). Its smallmouth counterpart was taken in Lake Champlain in 1978; it weighed 6 pounds, 12 ounces (3.06kg).

Lake Champlain is a must for anglers wanting to tackle Vermont bass, but other waters also recommended by the Vermont Fish and Wildlife Department include: Lake Dunmore, Lake Bomoseen, Lake St Catherine, Lake Fairlee, Lake Morey, Echo Lake, Woodward Reservoir, Harriman Reservoir, Somerset Reservoir, Connecticut River, White River, Winooski River, Otter Creek.

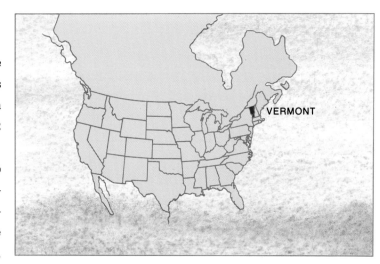

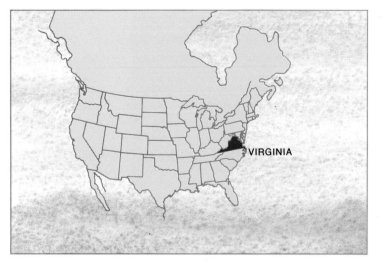

VIRGINIA

~

A largemouth bass set the State record of 16 pounds, 4 ounces (7.37kg) in 1985. It was taken in Lake Conners. Its counterparts are an 8-pound (3.6kg) smallmouth, caught in the New River in 1986, and a 6-pound, 10-ounce (3kg) spotted bass taken from Flannagan Reservoir in 1976.

WASHINGTON

~

Waters in this State that received top marks for bass in the 1990 Prospects report of the Washington Department of Wildlife were: Columbia River and its sloughs, Yakima River, Dry Lake, Sacajawea Lake, Silver Lake, Banks Lake, Leland Lake, Sprague Lake, Tee Lake, Washburn Island Pond, Whitestone Lake, Pend Oreille River, Sportsman Lake, Big Lake, Campbell Lake, Shoecraft Lake, Chapman lake, Clear Lake, Eloika Lake, Long Lake, Newman Lake, Munn Lake, ponds in the Bald Hills region of southern Thurston County, Cain Lake, Fazon Lake, Whatcom Lake, Wiser Lake.

State records: largemouth, 11 pounds, 9 ounces (5.25kg), 1977, Banks Lake; smallmouth, 8 pounds, 12 ounces (3.94kg), 1967, Columbia River.

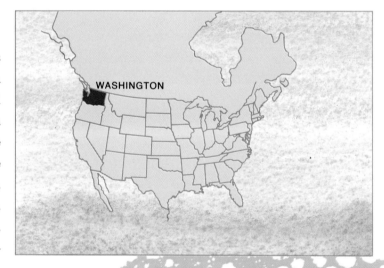

LEFT

*Lily pads attract many of
the bass's top food
choices, and hence many
nice bass.*

≈

WEST VIRGINIA

~

The State record largemouth is a 10-pound, 10-ounce
(4.82kg) fish caught in 1979 in Sleepy Creek Lake.
A smallmouth of 9 pounds, 12 ounces (4.44kg) set
its species' record when it was taken in 1971 in the
South Branch.

The spotted bass record stands at 3 pounds,
10 ounces (1.64kg), set by a fish hooked in 1988 in
R.D. Bailey Lake.

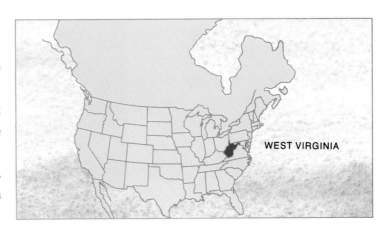

WEST VIRGINIA

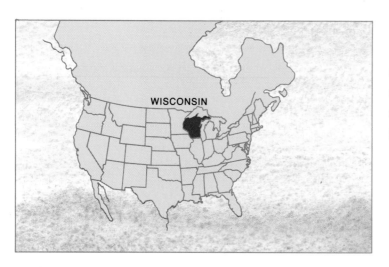

WISCONSIN

A largemouth bass of 11 pounds, 3 ounces (5.08kg) set the State record in 1940 on Lake Ripley. Its smallmouth counterpart was a 9-pound, 1-ounce (4.13kg) fish taken in 1950 in Indian Lake.

RIGHT

A bass's eye-view of the world above will vary, depending upon factors such as water clarity.

WYOMING

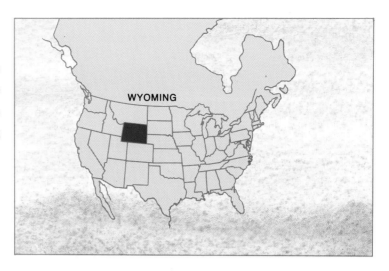

The State record largemouth is a 7-pound, 2-ounce (3.26kg) bass taken in 1942 on Stove Lake. The State record for smallmouth stands at 4 pounds, 12 ounces (2.16kg), set in 1982 by a fish taken from a mining pit in the southeastern part of the State.

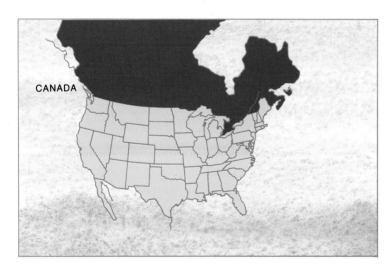

CANADA

Smallmouth bass have been introduced and taken hold in bodies of water throughout southern Canada, but they are far outshadowed in popularity by the enormous walleye, northern pike and salmonoid fisheries that this region has to offer. In many areas they are quite a recent introduction. Some areas that have received recent endorsements include: the lakes and streams of the St Croix, Magaguadavic and St John river drainages, North Lake, Skiff Lake, Loon Bay, the Grand Falls flowage, Eel River, First and Second Eel lakes, Mactaquac Lake, Lake Geoge, Harvey Lake, Big and Little Magaguadavic lakes, Oromocto Lake, Oromocto River, Lake Utopia and Digdeguash Lake in New Brunswick.

Smallmouth bass were first stocked into Nova Scotia's Bunker Lake in 1942. Subsequent introductions have established breeding populations in many of the Province's other lakes as well.

INDEX

BASS FISHING

96